W9-ADV-539

PORTO

STORIES FROM PORTUGAL'S HISTORIC BOLHÃO MARKET

GABRIELLA OPAZ AND **SONIA ANDRESSON NOLASCO**

PHOTOGRAPHY BY **RYAN OPAZ** FOREWORD BY **JOSÉ AVILLEZ**

S
SURREY
BOOKS

AN **AGATE** IMPRINT

CHICAGO

This book was first published in Portugal in 2016 by Oficina do Livro. This first U.S.
edition has been updated and redesigned.

Printed in China

Library of Congress Cataloging-in-Publication Data

Names: Opaz, Gabriella, author. | Andresson Nolasco, Sonia, author.
Title: Porto : stories from northern Portugal's historic Bolhão
  Market / Gabriella Opaz and Sonia Andresson Nolasco ; foreword by José
  Avillez ; photography by Ryan Opaz.
Other titles: Undiscovered food stories of northern Portugal
Description: First US edition. | Chicago : Surrey Books, an imprint of Agate
  Publishing, [2018] | Originally published under title: The undiscovered
  food stories of northern Portugal published in Portugal in 2016 by Oficina
  do Livro. | Includes index.
Identifiers: LCCN 2018007356 (print) | LCCN 2018010338 (ebook) | ISBN
  9781572848214 (e-book) | ISBN 1572848219 (e-book) | ISBN 9781572842564
  (hardcover) | ISBN 1572842563 (hardcover) | ISBN 9781572848214 (eISBN) |
  ISBN 1572848219 (eISBN)
Subjects: LCSH: Cooking, Portuguese. | Mercado do Bolhão (Porto, Portugal) |
  Porto (Portugal)--Description and travel. | LCGFT: Cookbooks.
Classification: LCC TX723.5.P7 (ebook) | LCC TX723.5.P7 O63 2018 (print) |
  DDC 641.59469/15--dc23
LC record available at https://lccn.loc.gov/2018007356

First U.S. Edition: August 2018

10 9 8 7 6 5 4 3 2 1   18 19 20 21 22

Surrey Books is an imprint of Agate Publishing. Agate books are available in bulk at
discount prices. Learn more at agatepublishing.com.

To the devoted, fearless, and loving vendors of Bolhão Market who have helped preserve the traditions and culinary tales of Northern Portugal. This book is our gift of gratitude to you, because through your voices, we found our own.

CONTENTS

RECIPES

FOREWORD
BY JOSÉ AVILLEZ

FAR FROM YOUR typical culinary tome or collection of trendy recipes, this is a book about people, lives, dreams, and desires. It's a book about identity and culture, a journey through Bolhão Market, one of the most emblematic food markets in Portugal—a discovery of local flavors and life stories.

In just the first few pages, we're immediately struck by the love and devotion with which the authors penned and adorned this book.

It's a book about love for Northern Portuguese cuisine. It transports our minds and makes our mouths water, while urging us to ponder the past and future of these people, and the impact that markets like this one have on our lives. It beckons us to consider what is bought and sold, produced and cooked, while unveiling recipes that are authentic pillars of this region's gastronomic culture. Passed down through the generations, these grandmother culinary secrets rarely rise from the sweet scribbles buried in their weathered notebooks or from the recesses of their minds.

This book takes us on a trip of discovery through the delectable nooks and crannies of the cuisine of the North, a land of warm hearts and brimming plates that we can vicariously touch and taste.

In these pages, we hear a piercing cry for the preservation of this ancient culture and the nourishing traditions that enrich the essence of the Portuguese. Traditions that are so significant to an identity and history, yet are sadly at risk of disappearing.

This book is undoubtedly a love letter to readers that are passionate about gastronomy, storytelling, history, and culture. It's for all of those who wish to feel and discover the spirit of the Nortenha (Northern) culinary identity.

Light the fireplace, grab a seat at the table—and savor.

Chef José Avillez is a Michelin-starred chef based in Portugal who focuses on contemporary Portuguese cuisine. His restaurant Belcanto earned its first Michelin star in 2012 and its second in 2014, and it has been recognized by the World's 50 Best Restaurants list multiple times. In addition to Belcanto, Avillez owns several other restaurants in Lisbon and one in Porto, and he has written five cookbooks. With a passion for innovating and promoting his country's cuisine, he has put Portugal on the international culinary stage. In 2018, Avillez was awarded the Grand Prix de L'Art de La Cuisine by the International Academy of Gastronomy, making him the first Portuguese chef to receive the honor.

When not caring for every plant, animal, and vendor inside the market, Marília Brandão is providing the freshest of poultry as she has done for more than 50 years.

PREFACE

❧

SHE SAT WITH the aura of a sentinel, barely blinking or stirring under the tattered tarps and disintegrating walls of Porto's centenarian open-air market, Bolhão. Cloaked in a kaleidoscope of sweaters, Amélia Malheiro's white wiry hair stood on end as the light pooled around her torn, black gardening boots. Though statuesque, she remained observant and vigilant. A red leaf shuddered in a frenetic dance past her cane before soaring into the air and landing on a shallow puddle between us.

"Come here," she called to us, gesturing with her thick, craggy hand to get closer. Before we could answer, she reached to blanket our hands with her own, to caress and gently ease us into her presence. Her stance shifted from guard to grandmother, from stoic to embracing—a woman that would fight tooth and nail to protect you from your worst nightmares.

Smiling warmly, her eyes beamed with sweet delight and tenderness as she whispered, "How are my beautiful girls today? Tell me you've eaten. At least a bowl of soup . . . something to warm your belly and soul."

How do you not fall in love? How do you not feel as if the heavens opened to reincarnate your perfect grandmother deity? She's soft and warm with the fierce ruggedness of a panther, able to endure life's greatest struggles regardless of their intensity.

And quite honestly, we needed her . . .

As an American living in Portugal and a Portuguese living in America, we've both struggled to stay true to ourselves and our roots while reaching forward into the unknown. It's not easy to accomplish your passions and conquer your fears while straddling cultures, searching for pieces of your puzzle amid the confusion of never quite fitting in. But when you find someone who can see you, who can offer you shelter from your identity storm, the world suddenly feels safe. To connect with someone is one of the greatest gifts on earth.

As seagulls pecked at lone breadcrumbs and fishwives sang in the distance, she slowly let go of our hands, grinned from one eye, and whispered, "There's nothing quite like good food, is there? You always feel full."

That one line, that one single sentence set our souls on fire!

———

Though Amélia Malheiro, in her 80s, lets her daughter-in-law handle their souvenir business, her mere presence exudes tranquility and warmth as she serenely watches over the market.

For the last three generations, Bolhão Market has been the life force of Porto and, until recently, the engine that powered the North of Portugal.

Despite the dilapidated and dismissed century-old structure, or the vacant stands aching for new blood, the men and women of Bolhão Market pulse with life. For the last three generations, Bolhão Market has been the life force of Porto and, until recently, the engine that powered the North of Portugal. Many of the vendors were either born or died within its weathered walls. They nursed the sick, fed the forgotten, and served as a lifeboat to anyone in need. Their homegrown produce became key ingredients in five-star restaurants, their meat graced the tables of royals, and their bread fed hungry little bellies. They were your local therapists, healers, and chefs. And if there is one sage piece of advice these people have lived by, it's to simply care, to reach out and connect with anyone in their path.

This history and compassion is exactly what motivated our intense desire to craft this book and capture their stories before it was too late. While Portuguese newspapers piled with endless woes about the market's crumbling architecture, the voices of the vendors remained silent and unheard. Wrapped in a technicolor wardrobe of wool and cotton patterns, their appearance harkens to the past, a time before sleek, sterile supermarkets and behemoth malls. Their stories were considered obsolete and uninteresting, a chilling reminder of harder times.

We felt the opposite!

This place and these people are a treasure chest of knowledge and wisdom, but for years their fates have teetered on unstable ground. After more than three decades of disrepair and neglect, in late 2016 the city finally nailed down preliminary plans for a complete renovation of the market. However, nearly a year later, timelines and details remained sparse, leaving the vendors in a state of flux. Some of the eldest began to leave after enduring some of the harshest years at Bolhão, working under the barest of conditions. As of this book's writing, those staying were to be transferred to a temporary market at La Vie shopping center nearby Bolhão, while the historic market was scheduled to close for about two years of construction.

Safeguarding a place for these vendors in the renovated market is significant to the preservation of Bolhão's identity, because it's these people that embody the heart of the North. They're the reason why visitors from around the world keep saying, "Porto is amazing! The food is incredible and the peo-ple—the people are just so unbelievably kind." That's right: they are extremely generous and the food is delicious, but it's all of this and more because of places like Bolhão! Northern Portuguese cuisine has been shaped by people who have continued to grow their own produce, source their own meat, and share generations of unrivaled expertise since the market opened.

Are we passionate about this? Unbelievably so! In an age of globalization when home cooking is being replaced by convenience food, we'll fight to retain even a sliver of what Bolhão represents—pure authenticity.

We had the honor and privilege of interviewing the vast majority of the vendors in the market for this book. We've spoken to countless Portuguese food experts and traveled to far-off corners of the region to understand Northern Portuguese food culture. To everyone who has helped us along the way, a most heartfelt *obrigada*!

As you turn the page and begin your journey, please remember that this isn't your traditional cookbook, coffee table book, or culinary anthropology. Among the stories and photographs in this book, you'll find a handful of carefully selected recipes that offer you a glimpse into the culinary tapestry of Northern Portugal. Since most are grandmother recipes, they're meant to be explored and experimented with—serving as a cultural touchstone to Portuguese gastronomy. Our goal is to have you feel, to break open your senses and taste, smell, and see life in a different way. We tend to detach from those around us, sheltering ourselves from the discomfort, pain, and confusion of life. Here and now, we invite you to do the opposite. We invite you to step into the lives of these resourceful and resilient individuals, the flowing contours of the land, the juicy flesh of their fruits, and simply feel Northern Portugal.

NORTHERN PORTUGAL

Atlantic Ocean

Minho River

Viana do Castelo

Lima River

4

Braga

Porto

1 **2**

Vila Real

3

Gaia

Douro River

Ovar

6

Aveiro

Viseu

PORTUGAL

You Must Taste...

1. Porto
Francesinha
Sardinhas
Tripas à moda do Porto
Éclair

2. Vila Nova de Gaia
Vinho do Porto
Broa de Avintes

3. Douro
Vinhos
Cerejas & Figos
Amêndoas

4. Minho
Arroz de Pato
Bacalhau
Caldo Verde
Vinho Verde

5. Trás-os-Montes
Alheira
Carne Barrosã
Porco Bísaro
Queijo Terrincho
Cabrito Assado
Azeitonas

6. Ovar
Pão de Ló

Illustration: José Miguel Carvalho Cardoso

INTRODUCTION

Porto's Bolhão Market: An Ode to the North

❦

IN THE QUAINT fishing village of Afurada, a squat middle-aged woman with the calves of an ox bends over to grab an armful of clean laundry. Her apron is soaked from the overflowing stone tank at the communal washhouse, but she's unperturbed. The day is warm and sunny, and despite the cool Atlantic winds, she expertly pins her patterned sheets on the clotheslines banking the river. By afternoon, they'll be permeated with the comforting aromas of sea, salt, and grilled fish.

The charming little villages dotting the Portuguese landscape are an integral part of the North's collective culinary psyche. They are human and cultural time capsules, guarding traditions, customs, and recipes. From the river communities of Minho, the undulating terraces of the Douro River, and the sleepy hamlets of Trás-os-Montes and Alto Douro, these villages have indelibly shaped Porto's cuisine.

Dubbed the "emerald province," Minho's grandeur lies in its verdant landscapes, with the Peneda-Gerês National Park as its crown jewel. Though architecture and natural beauty are magnetic draws, there's nothing quite like the richness of the food to entice a visit. There, you'll find the roots of the country's iconic *caldo verde* (kale or collard greens soup), its distinct Vinho Verde (green wine), and countless recipes that range from rustic duck rice and river eel to cod and hearty meat stews. It's a playful mash-up between coastal and mountain cuisines that seamlessly weaves its way into Porto and the Douro from the south and into Trás-os-Montes from the east.

The magnificent Douro Valley is not only where the two godly nectars of the North—Port and Douro wines—are produced, it's the perfect embodiment of Portuguese ingenuity. The Douro is rightly considered a wonder of nature, a testament to its contrasts and contours. The river extends for 557 miles through Iberia, carving its way from the Portuguese border to the Atlantic, where it reaches Porto. On its journey, the rushing river has sculpted a meandering path of folded hills and valleys draped in terraced vineyards—a vertiginous vertical landscape of astounding beauty. This masterpiece may solely seem the work of Mother Nature, but it's the explosive engineering crafted by cunning and innovative Portuguese minds that has truly set this region apart—an endearing trait of the Portuguese called *arte do desenrasca*, the art of making things work. These days growers have implemented easier methods for

Call it Oporto as visitors do, Porto like the Portuguese, or Invicta (undefeated) like a local, the country's second largest city influenced the name Portugal.

Left to Right:

Since 2001, the Douro Valley has been recognized as a UNESCO World Heritage Site; Touriga Franca is the most widely planted Port wine grape in the Douro Valley.

planting their vines, but originally, they turned to dynamite to tame the valley. They blasted the schist, the metamorphic rock that forms the hills, to create steps that served as flat terrain for planting.

The remote mountainous region of Trás-os-Montes (behind-the-mountains) is by far the most mystical of the Northern regions. Its rugged lands were occupied by numerous tribes, like the Romans and the Celtiberians, who imprinted their pagan and Catholic rituals on the area's multicultural fabric. Instruments like the *gaita de foles Mirandesa* (Portuguese bagpipe) are a nod to Trás-os-Montes's Celtic ancestry. When played from soaring mountaintops, the continuous legato sound would resonate across the land as an impending warning to both friends and foes. You'll also find the last remnant of the ancient language of the Kingdom of León—founded in AD 910 when the Asturian princes transferred their capital city from Oviedo to the city of León. The region included the entire northwestern quarter of the Iberian Peninsula until 1139, when Portugal seceded to become the independent Kingdom of Portugal. Though sparsely spoken, Mirandês is still considered Portugal's purest language.

The region's mysticism has equally seeped into its textured gastronomy, often divided between Terra Fria (Cold Land) to the north and Terra Quente (Hot Land) to the south. Terra Fria is renowned for its culinary diversity and ingredients. There, you can taste mouthwatering cured meats as well as Terrincho, a semisoft cheese made from the milk of the local Churra breed of sheep; earthy chestnuts and wild mushrooms; and premium meats from the native *porco Bísaro* (Bísaro pig) and the *boi Mirandês* (Mirandês ox). Terra Quente is widely known for its stifling hot summers. It's also home to Mirandela, most recognized for its smoked sausage dish, *alheira de Mirandela*; succulent cherries from Alfândega da Fé; spicy olive oils; and delicate almonds.

Beyond the silkiest sardines and sweetest shrimp sourced directly from the Atlantic, Porto also draws its culinary inspiration from the south, where neighboring villages and towns usher in the Center region. Ovar's *pão de ló*, for instance, can often be savored in neighborhood *tascas* (taverns) and restaurants. The pillowy, gooey cake is one of the *doçaria conventual* (convent sweets)—a throwback to when nuns and monks were intricately involved in developing Portugal's gastronomic heritage (see Pastries & Coffee on page 189).

Porto's food culture is profoundly rooted in these regional grandmother recipes. And no other place embodies this spirit more organically than the city's oldest open-air market, Mercado do Bolhão (pronounced bowl-YOW). For more than a century, merchants from across the vast Northern regions have united here to share their freshest ingredients, artisanal secrets, and compelling life stories. Long before António Correia da Silva designed the market in 1914, the grounds functioned as an open courtyard for people to sell their goods. Similar markets were scattered throughout the city, instigating the need for a central location to congregate, commune, and naturally, consume! The name Bolhão (which means "big bubble") was inspired by a spring believed to run underneath the land on which the stunning neoclassical building now sits—a structure that has retained much of its original splendor. A grand stone staircase is traced by wrought iron banisters, exalted domes soar above the city, and mythical sculptures sit regally on high. Like a revered duchess vaunting a tattered gown, Bolhão still has a visceral and palpable grandeur. It drips from every column and emanates from every window. It's unmistakably unique.

Don't be shocked if you stumble upon a pile of frosted phallic pastries in the city of Amarante, or mounds of pumpkin-stuffed pito *cakes (psst . . .* pito *means a woman's honeypot) in Vila Real—sex and food are considered the perfect pairing in Portugal.*

With its lush green valleys, rolling hills, and snaking vines, Minho is by far one of the most enchanting regions of Portugal.

For more than a century, Bolhão Market, an open-air market that nurtures both the region and its people, has been the heart and soul of Northern Portugal.

Porto is the antithesis of sterile; it's a continuous collage of colors, textures, patterns, and personality.

For decades, this market was the communal playground for the city, the place where everyone came for fresh fish, juicy gossip, and courting cards for beautiful young vendors. It was a village unto itself, a self-sustaining organism that breathed excitement. It pumped with life, coursed with activity, and drew in people from across the entire region. It was *the* place to be, a magnet of hope and the heartbeat of Porto. But with the advent of supermarkets, and the increase in automobile ownership, came the proliferation of convenience and the mindset that time is against us. Independent merchants specializing in high-quality products were replaced by megamalls that offered similar products at cheaper prices. It's the age-old story of mass consumption trumping sustainability. And nothing suffered more than Bolhão.

A market that was once 400 vendors strong now has fewer than 100. A place where vendors stood elbow to elbow and customers rubbed shoulders vying for fresh produce is desolate and empty. Metal scaffolding protects bypassers from falling plaster, tattered tarps are patched with makeshift plastic, and worn posters hide vacant stands. As is true in many parts of the world, politics played a cruel game with the market's future, leaving a wake of false promises and empty hope. Restoration and renovation were touted across newspaper headlines for decades, but nothing came of it. Vendors were forbidden to pass on their licenses, new customers became an infrequent sighting, and the structure crumbled in forgotten dreams.

What three decades of turbulence hasn't changed is the soulfulness of Bolhão's remaining people. On the mezzanine, amid grandmother vendors poring over their pyramids of produce, butchers hauling entire ox carcasses into their shops, and a knife grinder sending piercing squeals into the atmosphere as dull blades strike steel, there's a woman with a dazzling smile. Despite her full-time job, she still comes to the market daily to keep her mother's souvenir stand alive. The retro Manteigaria do Bolhão, a butter shop, is run by a widow in homage to her husband, who devoted his entire life to the market. On the ground floor, fishwives still enrapture passersby with their provocative pitches, street cats nibble up forgotten scraps, and nurturing pork goddesses fill intestines with herbed meats. As mouthwatering aromas of grilled chicken and charred red snapper swirl in the air, customers eagerly seek out everything from shredded kale and octopus to fresh herbs and spices.

Bolhão is more than a market; it's an identity. It's a cultural reference and a strong brand that connects the city to the near and faraway places that supply it. We know because we've visited these places. We've roamed the scraggy streets of Avintes on the other side of the Douro River, where a husband and wife duo wake up at the crack of dawn to craft their *broa de Avintes* (cornmeal and rye bread), the very same way their family has been making it for decades.

This dedication and devotion to one's work is an intrinsic part of the Portuguese culture. The Portuguese hide a powerful engine of productivity behind a wall of quiet humility. Their awe-inspiring feats and accomplishments are often swept under the rug, shrugged off as merely part of their cultural duty to forge ahead. Boasting is not part of their DNA, because for every accomplishment, there's a small internal voice that whispers, "I can do better."

Like the sand in the ocean, the Portuguese shift with the current. They fuse with their surroundings, adapt to change, and welcome the future. Despite thousands of men lost at sea, nearly 50 years of darkness under António Salazar's dictatorship, colonial wars, economic distress, and mass emigration, the Portuguese remain some of the most loving and gracious people on the planet. And there's no greater expression of their hospitality than through their food. Ever sit tableside in a Portuguese home? Wear elastic, because you're in for a three-hour food frenzy. There's always more! And when you think it's over and can't possibly eat another bite, sit back, breathe, and expand your stomach for an elephant-size portion of whatever hasn't been polished off. Because what history hasn't erased, crushed, or diminished is a deep and profound sense of sharing. You cannot survive isolation, oppression, and poverty without the strength and love of your community. They feel what you feel, and if they can't help you, they'll contact one of their 10 million cousins to saddle up and lend a hand. Which is why the Portuguese feel so

Food stories are so strong in Porto that residents are called Tripeiros (Tripe Eaters), harkening to the legend of *tripas à moda do Porto*. During the Age of Discovery, locals shipped their top meats to soldiers battling in Africa, leaving them behind with merely the *tripa* (entrails) to make their signature stew.

The Douro River is a beloved destination for families keen to escape the summer heat.

One of the most defining and charming aspects of Porto is its never-ending rainbow of ceramic *azulejos* (tiles).

profoundly connected to their roots, their *terra* (the origin), the place where home begins. It's not uncommon to be gifted with a bag of lemons from a grandmother's orchard or a jug of a neighbor's homemade olive oil. The *terra* is where you cook over an open hearth, pluck an orange off a tree, or meet up with family at the countless gastronomic festivals dedicated to cherries, cured meat, olive oil, and oh so much more. Bolhão represents these Portuguese foodie principles.

Despite not entirely escaping the pressures of globalization with some imported products on the shelves, Bolhão is abundant in regional treasures of all kinds. More than an open-air market, it's a historical monument and a place to source old stories. Bolhão is a philosophy that stands for an impassioned lifestyle and a sense of sustainability that extends far beyond its four walls. This is why we couldn't restrict our tale solely to the market. Like an ancient olive tree, we couldn't just speak to its sweet fruits or knotted bark; we needed to follow its roots to understand what gives it life, nourishment, and soul.

Let this book inspire you to delve deeper and fully savor Portuguese food culture. But let us forewarn you that other than its sexy seafood, homestyle Portuguese cooking wouldn't win any pageants. Similar to the soul food recipes of the American South, traditional Portuguese cuisine has been shaped by honest and practical cooking. It's comfort food made from "scrappy" ingredients that are bursting with flavor, stories, and love. Like with anything in life, necessity is the mother of invention, and the people who struggle the most are often the ones that create mind-blowing (or in this case, mouthwatering) solutions.

And there's no other place in Porto that embodies the Portuguese trait of making do with what's available more than Bolhão Market, one of the most authentic and welcoming places for people from all over the world to visit. It's also the purest place to feel and understand Porto's Tripeiro spirit of resilience, liberty, and generosity.

Thick planks of *bacalhau* (cured codfish) hang over the door of a *mercearia* (specialty food shop), where you can find authentic Portuguese foodie souvenirs to take home.

CUISINE HISTORY

Cornered by the Atlantic on one side and Spain on the other, the Portuguese could easily have spent their existence hiding in the shadows. Instead, they transformed their isolation into an opportunity, their confines into an occasion to create, adapt, and survive. And though circumstance may make Portugal feel nonexistent at times, and the rest of the world may consider it an afterthought, the people's deeply rooted sense of discovery keeps them testing their own limits time after time.

Who hasn't heard of Vasco da Gama? He's a stronghold in every child's history book! He embodies adventure, diving into the unknown, and embracing whatever comes his way. Prince Henry the

Navigator created a maritime school that invented the unprecedented navigational tools that inspired some of the world's best navigators, including Bartolomeu Dias, Fernão de Magalhães (Magellan), and Pedro Álvares Cabral. Sailing uncharted seas, these men transformed Portugal into one of history's most powerful empires, and changed the world forever.

Beyond sea routes, the Portuguese discovered foods that Europe had never tasted before and shared their own cooking techniques and ingredients with the rest of the world. In Brazil, the Portuguese found sugarcane, potatoes, tomatoes, and bell peppers. In turn, Portugal introduced *bacalhau* (cured codfish), *feijoada* (bean stew), and *cachaça* inspired by *aguardente* (firewater) into the Brazilian way of life. Asia gave Portugal cinnamon, cloves, nutmeg, pepper, sweet oranges, rice, and tea. In Africa, the Portuguese were introduced to coffee beans, peanuts, chilies, pineapples, and more. If it weren't for the Portuguese in Goa, India might not have its intense curry sauces, which require chilies, nor would Portugal have adopted its *chamuça* finger food. We might even argue (and others do, too) that the Portuguese invented fusion cuisine, or at least played a major role in its existence.

And though Portuguese and Spanish cuisines do share Mediterranean and Moorish roots, with many of the same base ingredients, Portuguese food has its own unique fusion. Through vast global explorations and widespread colonization, French invasions and British alliances, as well as mass emigration to nearly every dot on the map, the cuisine contains ingredient and spice combinations unseen elsewhere on the continent. It's this blend of Old and New World nuances that helps define Portuguese cuisine, coupled with their cleverness to create unlikely combos like *carne de porco à Alentejana* (pork and clams).

In each chapter, we pepper in pieces of this flavorsome Portuguese past, explaining the unexpected presence of exotic ingredients at Bolhão Market and in several recipes. It's one tasty travel!

Chamuças (a product of the Indo-Portuguese connection) are commonly enjoyed as a snack alongside a beer.

CHAPTER 1

BREAD

Helena Rosa Pereira
comes from a long line
of *broa* bakers from
Avintes, where baking is
part of the town's DNA.

16

"One reason the country breads of Portugal have such thick brown crusts and moist, chewy interiors is that they are baked at intense heat in brick or stone ovens filled with steam."

–JEAN ANDERSON, *THE FOOD OF PORTUGAL*

I N THE FADING light of the afternoon, the canopy gently flutters and flaps, announcing the arrival of a cool, gentle breeze. It's autumn, that time of the year when Bolhão Market fills its stands with a panoply of pumpkins, its restaurants with hearty soups, and its shelves with heaps of rich, flavorful bread. Helena Rosa Pereira smiles, brushes the flour from her muscled hands onto her apron, and continues with her story. "I have a very large family. At one point, practically a quarter of Avintes belonged to them, but now everyone has gone their separate ways," she says, standing tall and proud of her bread heritage. "*Broa de Avintes* was my familial bread. It was what my mother and father most baked at home."

Broa de Avintes is the most distinct of the *broas*, a category of cornmeal-based bread synonymous with the North of Portugal. The mother of these breads, *broa de milho*, originates from the lush lands of Minho and is the ultimate symbol of resilience, strength, and determination. While much of Portugal successfully grew wheat as a staple, the North, despite its ample rainfall, simply couldn't. Between its poor soils and incredibly harsh winters, wheat wasn't a viable option—but *milho* (corn) was! Thanks to the Age of Discovery, corn eased its way into the North to produce the iconic *broas* we can't get enough of today.

Through the years, these far-north bread recipes trickled down to the towns and villages in and around Porto and Vila Nova de Gaia, with nearby Avintes and Valongo taking up an important role in the region's baking history. There are several styles of *broa* (white, yellow, and dark), but the belle of the ball at

The tricky Portuguese word for bread, *pão*, can easily sound like *pau* (a stick or slang for a man's . . . ahem . . . pickle) if the nasal "ão" doesn't come through. Our handy tip: say "pound" without the "nd" at the end.

Bolhão is *broa de Avintes*. This incredibly dark, dense, and bittersweet bread is by far one of our favorites. What makes it unique is the combination of rye and cornmeal, with the occasional addition of malt, to produce a bread that's so rich and flavorful the smallest of nibbles will satiate you. It also happens to pair beautifully with both sweet and salty flavors. Hence, it's common to find the pear-shaped quince fruit transformed into a rich and tangy *marmelada* (jam) or with smoky grilled sardines topped on *broa*.

These *broas* are so beloved that some are even protected by the patriotic *confrarias* (brotherhoods) that the Portuguese created to preserve the origins of ingredients and methods of preparation used in all sorts of recipes. To be a member, you must be willing to don a campy outfit consisting of a wide-brim hat, a cape, and lots of ribbons and badges. Sexy? No. But it speaks volumes about their pride for their precious bread!

Admittedly, the Portuguese are bread worshippers, passionate experts in all things glutinous and doughy. Their adoration is visceral and genetic, a love that accompanies every meal, regardless of the hour, event, or occasion. It swallows fear, celebrates life, eases a conversation, and stimulates the senses. Bread is so central to Portuguese culture that entire festivals are dedicated to it, statues of bakers grace village squares, and museums are open with the sole purpose of showcasing the country's bread heritage. Back in the day, children even considered it a coveted gift. Bread represents more than food to the Portuguese; it symbolizes security, creativity, and identity.

This sense of identity is indelibly ingrained inside Bolhão, where people know exactly who bakes their bread each and every day. Helena Rosa's loaves are lovingly baked by her siblings, using age-old secret family recipes in the towns of Avintes, Gondomar, and Ribadouro. It's all extremely hush-hush.

Left to right:

Traditional baker at Padaria Arminda & Neto uses a bowl to knead the dough into a ball; the *broas* are placed on kale leaves before going into a wood burning oven; bakers remove the piping hot *broas* from the oven for sale.

Not all Portuguese breads are called pão. *Some sound like the Portuguese word for cake,* bolo, *due to their texture (e.g.,* bôla). *And not all foods called bread are actually bread. For example,* pão de ló *is a type of sponge cake.*

The mysticism surrounding Helena Rosa's family recipes is part of a bigger *broa de Avintes* inheritance, bursting with tradition and lore. All of Avintes moves to the beat of *broa*! And because of it, it's known as Terra da Broa (land of *broa*), a place where baking bread is ingrained in the people's DNA. Though there are mass-produced versions of *broa*, there are also plenty of bakeries in the area dedicated to artisanal baking. The secret of the *broa de Avintes* starts with a searing hot wood burning oven that is started well before dawn. As the embers gain a healthy red glow, the *massa velha* (old dough) is added to the newly mixed dough to initiate the natural fermentation process.

Once the dough has reached the desired consistency, it's handed off to an assembly line of bakers, all with their special role to play. One might be in charge of kneading each batch of dough into a ball, while another is dedicated to molding it into its characteristic bell tower shape before sliding it onto a wooden paddle and into a stone oven for approximately four hours. It's a true labor of love for these people of the North, who are proud to call this bread uniquely their own.

In Avintes, you won't be greeted by your stale and predictable "man on horse" monument—there it's all about *Á Padeira*, which depicts the *padeira de Avintes* (female baker of Avintes) who began selling bread at Porto's street fairs decades before Bolhão opened its doors. It's a tribute to these women's virtues (strength, willfulness, and grace), beautifully exemplified by their heroic journey across the Douro River. With a *giga* (basket) balanced precariously overhead and piled high with freshly baked *broa*—weighing up to 100 pounds!—these bakers would traverse down the steep embankment onto the docks where a *valboeiro* (traditional rowboat) would carry them over the choppy waves to Porto. From the Ribeira (a riverfront neighborhood), they would arduously climb the *escada das padeiras* (staircase of the bakers) rising from the river and trek it to the top of the hill and down winding narrow streets to various selling points throughout Porto. When the bustling city traffic hushed to a hum, they immediately took to the river to cast their captivating sales pitches to hungry fishermen. Perceptive, the *padeiras* were capable of smelling a sale from a mile away. As the Portuguese like to say, you "don't *fazer farinha* [make flour] out of these ladies." Essentially, they don't take crap from anyone! Today, you can still see the occasional *giga* precariously swaying overhead, but like all traditional customs, it's dissolving into stories nestled in fables and children's books.

As rich ambient scents from the sea hover lightly over her stand, Helena Rosa tells of the solace and strength she finds in her mother's past, once filled with a willful determination to deliver handmade *broa* into Porto as her ancestors had done more than a century ago. When Helena Rosa was three, she and her family would climb into a truck loaded with heavy cargo and watch their overstuffed baskets of bread bounce and weave down cobblestone roads from Avintes into the heart of Porto.

"I was so small that all I remember seeing was my mother's skirt as I held on to it the entire way," Helena Rosa says. "My mother used to unload her baskets at the bus depot in Batalha [a neighborhood in Porto], while entrusting me to a friend as she ran around the city delivering her goods. When the baskets became too heavy to carry, she jumped on a trolley. She spent most of her life carrying baskets of bread on her head, because we didn't have a stand."

Despite her younger years on the city streets, the majority of Helena Rosa's existence has been lived within the tight-knit community of Bolhão. It became her home, filled with people she considers family. It was, and still is, a safe and loving place where children are taught to be strong, assertive, and savvy—a place where instinct rules. She adores the liberty children have inside Bolhão and how astute and sensitive they've become. "When my daughter was three, she would come with me to the market every day, and when we arrived at the door, I would point up the street and say, 'When you turn four, you're going to school up there,'" says Helena Rosa. "And before I knew it, my daughter grabs a bus by herself and gets off in front of the school, walks in, and says, 'I'm the daughter of Rosa the baker, and I'm coming to school.'"

Bolhão isn't for helicopter moms and doting parents. The community values gumption and precociousness. It raises children who know what they want and find resourceful ways to get it. You can't help but feel heaps of respect.

Around the holidays, especially Easter, Helena Rosa and her peers will line their counters with the stuffed breads of the North, a staple of holy festivities. If you're ever welcomed into a Northern home (it's highly likely), chances are you'll be greeted with small bites of this bread moistened with a mixture of mouthwatering meats, *bacalhau*, or sardines paired with a glass of wine. Called either a *bôla* or *folar*, the shape of these breads varies by region, but generally the former resembles a loaf and the latter a cake. They're ideal for picnicking or quick snacks when traveling with kids. Some of the most

Bolhão's bread vendors offer up a series of traditional cakes during the holidays, including Portuguese fruit cake, the *bolo rei*.

popular meat recipes come from the far-north villages of the Douro, Minho, and Trás-os-Montes, where artisanal bread baking is a way of life. Among the steep, terraced vineyards of the Douro Valley, you'll find the picturesque village of Favaios propped high on a plateau. If you're a lover of rustic breads and sweet Moscatel dessert wine, this is the place to visit. The village's adoration of this idyllic pairing runs so deep that it has even created a museum called Museu do Pão e do Vinho de Favaios (Bread and Wine Museum of Favaios).

Favaios bread is a rare creature not only because of its age-old baking technique, deep within wood burning ovens, but also for its distinct bow tie shape. Taking a hand-size ball of dough, the baker expertly twists and turns it before halving it in the Favaios fashion of keeping two small oval pieces connected through a mere starchy string. The traditional technique gives the two pieces of dough breathing room, resulting in lighter loaves that retain their airy interior for days on end.

Beyond crusty and meaty loaves, the Portuguese concoct entire dishes out of their bread. Portugal's queen of smoked sausage, *alheira*, is a prime example of the Portuguese manipulation of bread in meals. Stuffed not only with *pão de trigo* (wheat bread), tons of garlic, game meats, and pork, this sausage is also jam-packed with intrigue. What appears as normal, everyday Portuguese sausage is believed to have been invented by the Portuguese Jews (a.k.a Sephardic Jews) to escape the wrath of the Inquisition.

As the story goes, when the practice of the Jewish faith was outlawed during this period, entire Jewish communities (a significant number in Trás-os-Montes) were forced to convert to Christianity as Cristãos Novos (New Christians). In most cases, this was a mere disguise as Jews continued to practice their religion underground. The trick was appearing to partake in the common practices of Christianity, which included making and enjoying smoked pork sausages that hung from the *fumeiros* (smokehouses). To keep their cover, the Jews created *alheira* using a pork-free blend of game meats laced with mounds of bread and garlic. The counterstory is that this sausage was simply developed by those who couldn't afford pork, thereby creating a sausage stuffed with whatever they had on hand.

Whatever the truth may be, one thing's for sure—the Portuguese adore *alheira* and so do we. The most renowned come from Vinhais and Barroso-Montalegre in the Trás-os-Montes region and have an IPG (Product of Geographic Indication) seal of approval. The popular dish of *alheira de*

Alheira, the decadent bread, garlic, and game sausage of the North, is believed to have been invented by Portuguese Jews to fool the Inquisition.

Mirandela—sausage deep fried and served with French fries, egg, and a side salad—is one of the top winter-friendly foods you can enjoy. It's the kind of dish the Portuguese save for when they're feeling gastronomically sinful.

Interestingly, *alheiras* weren't traditionally produced in Mirandela. The town was merely a drop-off point for many Transmontanos (people of Trás-os-Montes) that shipped their product to Porto by train, and from there to the rest of the country. Since *alheira* is made from perishable ingredients, it's important to note that it isn't eaten like a charcuterie product—it should be thoroughly fried, grilled, or boiled. And of course, it's fantastic stuffed inside—you guessed it—bread!

Another savory speciality is *açorda*. This bread-based stew originated in the Southern region of Alentejo but is now served across the country, albeit with regional twists. In an *açorda à Alentejana*, chunks of leftover bread are tossed into a flavorful broth of garlic, olive oil, and fresh coriander, with an egg gently placed on top to poach. Intriguingly, there are definite similarities between *açorda* and the Arab dish *tharid*, made with pieces of bread in a vegetable or meat broth. As a result of the Moorish (medieval Arab) occupation in the Iberian Peninsula, lasting centuries, it's no wonder that the Portuguese adopted an imaginative and delicious repurposing of bread. In Trás-os-Montes, you can test your culinary limits by tucking into a nice big bowl of pig's brain *açorda* from the village of Medrões—seconds anyone? The recipe combines leftover bread with *mioleira* (pig's brain), shredded ribs, onion, garlic, white wine, olive oil, pepper, and parsley. If you're looking for a slightly tamer version, you can find everyone's favorite—the *açorda de marisco*. Made with a medley of delectable shellfish from the Portuguese coast, you can taste it in several restaurants throughout Porto.

A sweet contrast to these intense savory flavors is *pão doce* (sweet bread), which comes in a never-ending variety of shapes and sizes. In some parts of the North, it's traditional for godparents to give godchildren a sweet bread on Easter called *regueifa doce*, seasoned with fennel and cinnamon (nonsweet versions are also available). Sometimes called *pão Espanhol* (Spanish bread), the *regueifa* is

Left to right:

A *meia de leite* (milk and espresso) with Portugal's brioche-style croissant; the ubiquitous *tosta mista* (pressed ham and cheese toast); *regueifa* bread loaves piled up at Bolhão Market.

The eldest of the bread vendors at Bolhão, Maria Madalena Machado has dedicated more than half of her life to the market.

From crusty loaves and buttery *broas* to puffy rolls, Bolhão Market is a terrific place to taste a variety of Portuguese breads.

tied to Portugal and Spain's Al-Andalus (Islamic Iberia) roots. The term derives from the Arabic word *rghaif*, referring to folded dough, a distinguishing characteristic of this bread. In Porto today, you can find a plethora of sweet bread year-round. It's common, for example, to have buttered *pãezinhos de leite* (sweet rolls) for breakfast. As a matter of fact, Portugal's traditional croissant is a type of sweet bread that's similar to a brioche, as opposed to the flaky, Vienna-style pastry (sometimes also available).

The market is a terrific place to sample a variety of these breads without committing entirely to one large loaf—customers can buy as much or as little as they like. This not only benefits the tourist on a mission to experiment, but it's also a worthwhile way of valuing sensible consumption over pre-packaged convenience, massification, and waste. In times of economic crisis, it's also budget friendly. These are topics near and dear to Maria Madalena Machado, the eldest of the bread vendors at the market.

"This is a *regueifa* and I can sell it to you whole, half, or by the kilo," she explains, pointing authoritatively to a billowy baguette hanging among its brethren.

Amid rustic loaves encased in rupturing crusts, Maria Madalena's stand is stocked daily with an assortment of rolls, piled up like puffy pillows behind the glass. This is Portugal's ordinary sandwich bread, ideal to stuff with *queijo* (cheese) and *presunto* (cured ham). It's the kind of bread mothers always have handy for their children's after-school snacks. Though commonly called a *papo-seco* or *carcaça* throughout the country, these rolls have a few other names in Porto. At the market, you might hear *molete*. Some believe the name derives from a French officer, General Moulet, who during the French invasions of Valongo ordered smaller bread to be baked due to a grain shortage. Others claim there's a Castilian influence, tied to the word *mole* (soft), the main characteristic of this bread.

In a military stance that complements her crisp lab coat, short grey hair, and simple glasses, Maria Madalena rips apart today's supermarket practices. What used to be a trade passed on from generation to generation has now diffused into a one-stop-shopping mentality. "The same person that shreds your

Left to right:

Soft or crusty, bread rolls in Portugal are key to its mouthwatering sandwiches; don't miss the garlicky juice-dripping *bifana* (fried pork sandwich) at Conga; the rustic *terylene* slow-roasted pork and cured ham specialty at Flor dos Congregados.

kale and weighs your potatoes also makes omelets," she says. In the past, she adds, only certain places were allowed to sell bread. It was a question of pride and expertise.

She interrupts our conversation to vanish behind the counter in search of a certificate. The pause allows us to pick out the grassy scents coming from the next stand, where a slender blonde is barely visible behind gallon-size buckets of green, burgundy, and black olives. The thought of pairing Maria Madalena's cornmeal loaves with the tiny, briny fruit is tantalizing and distracting. Our stomachs grumble . . .

Maria Madalena returns with a laminated certificate from 1966. It's a testimony to her years as a Milaneza employee, and an obvious point of pride. She was on the team that introduced Milaneza's brand of bread, *pão Milaneza*, into the Porto bread scene in 1959. Owned by Cerealis, a food producer founded in 1919 in the city of Maia, Milaneza is one of Portugal's top pasta brands, selling throughout the country and around the globe. With enough bread and business expertise under her belt, Maria Madalena eventually left the company and opened the stand where she has remained until this day, a place where professionalism and quality remain core to her being.

Of the 80 some-odd years Maria Madalena has graced our planet, more than half have been spent in the market. Today, most of us can't hold a job for more than a decade. But when she fell ill a few years ago, she passed the reins to her daughter Maria Amélia Babo. Understandably, Maria Madalena can't stay away from the market entirely: the draw is too intense, her identity is too integrated. Those brief moments at the market provide a touchstone for her soul to rekindle what she has spent so long creating—a home.

When inspiration hits, Maria Madalena fancies penning short poems (sometimes political) and pastes them on her stand's window to make a statement. Rumor has it that poorly behaved customers (men and women) have been set straight by Maria Madalena—and not just verbally. But get past her deep commanding voice and stern demeanor, and you'll discover a sweet soul who is quite a comedian. And like most of the vendors at the market, once she gets to know you, she treats you like family.

"At the market, customers become friends," she tells us as an elderly woman slips her a grocery bag. The woman does this regularly to stroll the market hands-free, an unlikely occurrence outside a traditional market like this one. Clearly, Maria Madalena sells bread, but she also offers up kindness for free.

"We have to uplift people," she says. "Many women used to come here who had problems with their children and husbands; they liked to talk to me and get it off their chest." It's that same nurturing

Due to Portugal's vast microclimates, only certain cereals can flourish in particular areas. Thus, the bread in your hand—often named after its town of origin—tells a rich story based on its shape and ingredient.

Maria Madalena Machado pastes short poems on her stand window with positive messages about the market. This one encourages people to shop at Bolhão for true satisfaction.

element that we see time and time again in the market. A desire to care for others, to ensure that their well-being is fiercely guarded.

On the other side of the market, there's a bread vendor that would be a shoo-in for a beauty pageant. A sign above her stand says "No Pictures" in Portuguese, but how could one resist that Old Hollywood charm? Alzira Almeida e Silva is a hottie! Even in her silver years, she could rock a pinup calendar. Her natural elegance is topped with pretty mauve lipstick, and her neatly pinned bangs give way to faded blonde waves that blend into the rows upon rows of finely crushed homemade breadcrumbs behind her. A staple on all the bread vendors' shelves, they're used for making *salgados* (savory snacks) that range from *rissóis de camarão* (crescent-shaped shrimp turnovers) to *croquettes de carne* (meat croquettes). These repurposed breadcrumbs, made from day-old breads, are also essential in making *panados,* breaded foods often made with pork and turkey cutlets. Shove these babies inside a Portuguese roll, slap on a lettuce leaf and a dollop of mayo, and you've got yourself a traditional *sandes de panados.*

Though Bolhão has been her life since she was 14, Alzira might close up shop once the market goes into construction. It won't be an easy decision for her, so she's counting on her faith to keep her strong, and on God to ease her transition. She owns the stand that once belonged to her original employers, the very same people who supply her with bread today, including everyone's beloved *broa de Avintes.*

Left to right:

The *rissol* (turnover) is one of the most popular *salgados* (savory snacks) in Portugal. Here, it's stuffed with roasted, pulled suckling pig; Alzira Almeida e Silva started working at the market when she was 14.

Alzira recalls fondly the hustle and bustle of the market when there were 10 bread vendors in operation. Now, she's one of three.

Despite an increase in tourism, Alzira has seen a significant drop in sales. Staring at her hands, she fondly remembers Saturdays in which she sold 6,000 loaves. Sit with that number for a moment: 6,000. Today, she's lucky if she sells 100. With such a low number, and years of working her hands to the bone, it's hard to keep her stamina going and retain that excitement. As her bright eyes tear up, she says, "Maybe I'll go travel a bit of the country. I like the beach." Though her words are genuine, the result may not be the same as the intention. Years ago, Alzira embarked on a minivacation to Praia da Nazaré (a beach town an hour's drive north from Lisbon), but after a few days she rushed back to Bolhão. "I missed it and wasn't able to unwind," she says. "So you can see how important Bolhão is to me."

It goes beyond the bread for these women. Selling at the market gives them a chance to do what Portuguese women do best—care for others. Step into any traditional Portuguese home and you'll surely be showered with a buffet of cheese, jams, cured meats, and olives, all with bread as the centerpiece. In the Fado (Portuguese blues) song "Uma Casa Portuguesa" ("A Portuguese Home"), the lyrics say that in a Portuguese home bread and wine are a must, and when there's a knock on the door, insist that the guest sit at the table. This scenario comes with a promise of kisses and arms flung wide open to greet you. The warming scents of bread inside Bolhão are a reminder of the joy bread brings to the Portuguese and the people they share it with.

When sitting down to a meal at a restaurant take note that the appetizing display of bread, olives, pâté, and cheese is not free! Called a *couvert*, it's the Portuguese way of ensuring your palate is constantly swimming in flavors.

Right:

Broa de Avintes (cornmeal and rye bread) on display at Bolhão Market.

OLIVE OIL & WINE

Olive oil and wine are two of the greatest gastronomical gifts Portugal has bestowed upon the planet. They're so ubiquitous that it's nearly impossible to enjoy a meal without them—and quite frankly, we don't suggest you try! They're used to marinate roasts, flavor soups, and sneak their way into desserts. Like their Mediterranean kin, they're also used to lubricate conversations and heal the sick. In short, *azeite* (olive oil) and *vinho* (wine) course through Portuguese cuisine, giving it richness and life.

For those keen to seek out a Northern Portuguese wine, look no further than Vinho Verde and the Douro. Vinho Verde hails from the lush, verdant lands of Minho, hence the literal translation of its name, "green wine." A more accurate translation might be "young wine," as it has gained international attention for its fresh, effervescent white wines. But don't limit yourself, because many of these wines can age beautifully, showing incredible depth, concentration, and elegance. In the Douro Valley, the world's first demarcated wine region, you can find both still and fortified wines as well as a handful of *espumantes*, or sparkling wines. If you've never visited, book a trip, because it's by far one of the most breathtaking landscapes in the world. Rounded folds of terraced vineyards rise up from the river, creating an almost extraterrestrial landscape. Paired with the intoxicating aroma of dried figs and toasted almonds in a 20-year tawny Port wine, the experience borders on orgasmic.

While its cousin Spain still surpasses Portugal in both consumption and production, the beauty of Portuguese olive oil lies in its artisanal producers. These small but mighty growers from the Trás-os-Montes and Alto Douro are crafting aromatic and elegant extra virgin olive oils. Replete with vibrant aromas, such as green grass, raw almond, tomato leaf, banana, walnut, and artichoke, they're perfect to drizzle on heirloom tomatoes or to soak up with a hunky piece of warm crusty bread. For the purist eager to savor the juicy *azeitonas* (olives) that predominantly produce Northern Portuguese olive oil, seek out madural, negrinha do freixo, verdeal, and cobrançosa—a wonderful accompaniment to a glass of Vinho Verde!

In the market, you'll find a few examples of olive oil and wine, but for a crash course head to Rua Ferreira Borges. On this street, you'll not only find Oliva & Co., a shop dedicated to Portuguese olive culture, but also Wines of Portugal located inside the Palácio da Bolsa (Stock Exchange Palace) for still wines; the Instituto dos Vinhos do Douro e Porto just up the road for fortified wines; or PROVA right across the street for wines by the glass.

Never heard of Portuguese olive oil? Then you're in for a delightful experience!

OUR FAVORITES

Alheira

Shrouded in mystery, *alheira* deserves to be enjoyed in a romantic setting. Hidden among a labyrinth of quiet cobbled alleys sits one of the most enchanting restaurants in Porto, Flor dos Congregados. It's an ode to the Middle Ages with protruding stone walls, gargantuan wooden structures, and enough cozy warmth to make your grandmother's house seem sterile—except for the dining room chairs, which kinda feel as if you're sitting on wooden seesaws. For more than 160 years, Flor dos Congregados has garnered a stunning reputation for its traditional slow-cooked food. Whether you prefer your bread sausage laced with pork or game meats, this is the ideal place in the city to experience the rustic, rich, and succulent *alheira*—perfect to pair with a Douro red and steaming bowl of *caldo verde*, or kale soup.

Broa de Avintes

If you are a die-hard foodie, rent a car and head to Avintes. This vine covered village, located just a stone's throw from the city of Vila Nova de Gaia, is home to the moist and bittersweet *broa de Avintes*. For generations, family-run bakeries like Padaria Arminda & Neto have been crafting artisanal *broas* from wood burning ovens—the very same ovens that are slowly dying out in favor of their electric cousins. Our suggestion: get to the bakery bright and early to enjoy a piping hot loaf while chatting up the grandmothers convening for their daily dose of gossip. Or find a willing Portuguese speaker (give us a ring!) to reserve a *chouriço-* (smoked sausage) filled *broa*. This incredibly dark, dense, and delicious bread packed with juicy, spiced meat is gorgeous when served warm and even better when paired with *espumante*.

Bôla de Carne

This soft, pan-baked wheat bread is made with a variety of stuffings depending on the region, which is why you should try it everywhere! A quick find is at the market or the bakeries around Porto, but for something hardcore traditional, place an order with Padaria Central (or another local artisan bakery) on your visit to the Douro Valley's bucolic village of Favaios. The bakers slow cook regional meats, such as veal, chicken, cured ham, and smoked sausages, in rich olive oil infused with spices and bay leaf. Once the meats are tender, they're laid over stretched dough and topped with a second doughy layer before going into the oven. Cut into bite-size pieces, it's a wonderful snack with a glass of wine.

Salgados

If you have a salty tooth, *salgados* (savory snacks) will transport you to tasty breaded food heaven! From pudgy Portuguese aunts to upscale pastry shops, everybody makes them filled with, but not limited to, shrimp mousse, ground veal, and pulled chicken. They're a staple finger food at children's birthday parties, starters during the holidays, a small bite in the middle of the day, or an entire meal when paired with a salad or rice. Though ubiquitous, some places make them better than others. Taste test a few to find your favorite, but for a sure thing head to Porto's Confeitaria Petúlia for their spicy *rissóis de leitão* (suckling pig turnovers).

CHAPTER 2

FRUITS & VEGETABLES

During the Age of Discovery, the Portuguese introduced the sweet oranges they discovered in China and India to the rest of the world. This is why the word for orange in several countries is associated with Portugal. For example, an orange in Greece is *portukali*.

THE LUSH UNDULATING textures of the North extend far beyond its moss covered walls and green vines. Their raw power and will to survive breaks buildings, absorbs stone, and exemplifies the Portuguese's inherent ability to work hand in hand with Mother Nature.

Try walking the cobbled streets of Porto without seeing a head of cabbage or sprig of kale peeking out from behind cement walls. These tiny plots of land have always been a fantastic opportunity to reduce costs and eat sustainably by growing a wide variety of fruits and vegetables. When the bounty was ready, what wasn't consumed at home would overflow wicker baskets in a mélange of color to be sold in markets. Today, you won't find women sauntering through the streets in a Carmen Miranda fashion with baskets of fruit atop their heads, but the heritage still lives on in Bolhão. And if you're up for a little trivia, the Brazilian queen of fruit fascinators was actually born in Minho!

Patiently peeling the skin off pudgy, flecked beans buried in a plastic bag, Deolinda Santos Marques sits on a stool surrounded by crates bursting with fat, juicy tomatoes, vibrant string beans, and iridescent carrots, the showstoppers amid piles of produce. Despite her 80-plus years of wisdom, Deolinda is a powerhouse with massive, rugged hands that speak to the hard work and toil she has endured over the years. Selling produce has been her life, her gift, and occasionally, her passion.

A salt and pepper tousled bob is barely visible from under Deolinda's boonie hat, dark like the rest of her layered outfit of multipatterned shirts, cardigans, skirts, stockings, and leg warmers. As

"Portugal has a great soup tradition. It's not based on stocks, just cooking ingredients together."
—*Chef José Avillez*

If you're looking for the true essence of Portuguese *saudades*, sit with Deolinda Santos Marques, a woman with an endearing nostalgic nature.

seagulls claw on the railing, she sits quietly staring at some point in the distance. Having lost one of her sons less than a decade ago, her entire demeanor is that of mourning, longing, and empty distress. "If it weren't for this pain, I would have left Bolhão a long time ago, but coming here helps me," she says, wiping away a tear. "When our parents die, it's difficult, but it passes. When it's our child, the pain never goes away."

Just south of Porto, in the seaside town of Espinho, you'll find Deolinda selling her garden fresh produce. It's her Monday respite, filled with sun-kissed cheeks and orange sunsets. But more often than not, you'll find Deolinda fondly reminiscing of times gone by at Bolhão.

"When I was a child," Deolinda says, "I had one pair of clothes for the entire week and then another pair for Sunday. That was it." Maria da Conceição Pinto Ferreira, down a few stands from Deolinda, comes over to join the conversation.

"We were from a village up there [north of Porto], where a farmer had eight children including twin girls around my age. So, when it came time to have my First Communion, I borrowed clothes from them for my outfit," says Maria da Conceição, one of the busiest produce vendors at the market. She's almost impossible to catch as she shuffles back and forth between the front of the stand and her ever-ringing phone. If it weren't for her husband, getting a word in with her would be nearly impossible! From historic cafés like the Majestic and Guarany to the Montepio bank cafeteria, the list of restaurants Maria da Conceição supplies is long. Despite the wear and tear of the market, this vendor's verve for life is as strong as the roots of the fruits and vegetables she grows. The sun may not have always shined on these women, but when it did, they knew how to soak it up to sustain themselves through grimmer days. They are self-taught, savvy saleswomen. You wouldn't know it by how quickly Deolinda makes change and scribbles in her notebook, but she's illiterate. Or, as we see it—incredible!

Don't reach for the smooth Portuguese melão *(honeydew); instead look for intensely fragrant ones with roughened skins. Typically, these are ripe, sweet, and ready to savor!*

WASHINGTON-CENTERVILLE
PUBLIC LIBRARY
Date of checkout:
06/18/2022

Portugal.
Barcode: 33508016197876
DUE: 07-09-22

Portugal & the Azores [DVD] / Pilot Fi
Barcode: 33508009589212
DUE: 07-09-22

Porto : stories from Portugal's histor
Barcode: 33508014404654
DUE: 07-09-22

Number of items checked out: 3

You saved this much by using your
library today: $71.89

Washington-Centerville Public Library
(937) 433-8091
wclibrary.info

Maria da Conceição Pinto Ferreira supplies her succulent fruit and crisp vegetables to some of the most iconic cafés in Porto.

Left to right:

Medley of plump tomatoes; the meaty *coração de boi* (heart of bull) tomato.

"My son often says that he admires me," Deolinda says, "because when there was the currency change from *escudos* to euros, he was convinced that I would make mistakes. He brought me 10 *contos* [colloquial name for 10,000 *escudos*, Portugal's former currency] in coins, and I made change. He was dumbfounded and said I had to teach his daughters, because I knew more than they did." Deolinda smiles widely. "My mother, who passed away six months before her 100th birthday, didn't know how to read either, but nobody fooled her. My great-grandmother had a business, but like us she didn't know how to read. When people owed her money, she put a small circle by their name. The size of the circle corresponded to the amount they owed. She taught me her system and soon my mind began to open. From then on, I learned easily, and never messed up. I was never a dummy, thank God."

At Maria da Conceição's stand, we're introduced to the *tamarilho* or Brazilian tomato, a cross of a Roma tomato with traces of plum and passion fruit. As it grows well in her garden (several tropical fruits do in Portugal's temperate climate), she graces us with its exotic sumptuous flavor—to die for! For the sharp eye, there are heaps of rare treasures throughout the market. But if you're looking for the Portuguese workhorse, it's the domestic tomato that holds reign. Among a papery melee of greens, onion, and the occasional bell pepper, it's the diva tomato soaked in vinegar and olive oil that graces every meal. Especially luscious are the meaty *coração de boi* (heart of bull) tomatoes that need only a

While nuns whipped up egg creams for delicate pastries, monks taught Portuguese peasants the art of growing beautiful fruit.

sprinkle of coarse salt and drizzle of olive oil to delight your taste buds on hot summer days. Tomatoes and bell peppers are also thrown into many Portuguese sauces that start with a sauté called *esturgido* in the North, or a *refogado* in other parts of the country. The red bell pepper inspired the Portuguese to concoct a savory paste called *massa de pimentão*, an invention of the South that is now a staple condiment throughout Portugal.

Though there is certainly an abundance of fresh vegetables at the market, these are rarely the centerpiece of most dishes in Portugal. With the exception of legume salads and frittered vegetables, veggies play their biggest roles in rice pilafs, side dishes, stews, and soups. The pink spotted beans that Deolinda has been peeling throughout our conversation are destined for soups. "It's a wonderful way to create a creamier broth," she explains. Leave the skin on for rustic notes or melt bare beans like potatoes, creating a delicate creamy texture. Her beautiful green and purple string beans labeled *vagem*, another name for *feijão verde*, catch our eye. They're fat, smooth heirloom string beans with a meatier interior and a nuttier flavor than the ordinary type. They're used in Portugal as a side dish, boiled and garnished with minced garlic, vinegar, and olive oil. They're also slivered into the *sopa de feijão verde*, a velvety string bean soup—one of many in Portugal's impressive soup repertoire.

Left to right:

Buttery *feijão verde* (string beans); *salada de feijão frade* (black-eyed pea salad); shoppers seeking out Bolhão's fresh produce.

In fact, soups are the heart and soul of Portuguese cuisine. Whether to ward off cold winter nights or simply to savor on a sunny spring afternoon, soups are everywhere. Their purpose is threefold. First, they're a fast and efficient means of clearing out the fridge. What a casserole might be to an American, a soup is to a Portuguese. Second, they're the base nutrition to every child's upbringing. From the tender age of one, tiny hands instinctively grab for a spoon at mealtime. And third, they provide the entire nation with its recommended dose of veggies.

Take the queen of Portuguese soups, *caldo verde*, chock-full of vitamin E. This famous soup from Minho is made with a garlic potato puree, and strands of *couve Galega* (a Northern kale) and topped with rounds of *chouriço* (smoked sausage) and drizzles of olive oil. You'll also see the soup made with collard greens. Historically, struggling families—especially rural—made their soups as robust as possible to compensate for their protein ration of pork belly or sardines, while wealthier tables savored bisques ladled in Vista Alegre porcelain on hand-embroidered tablecloths. Fortunately for us, modernity has yet to erase the Portuguese love of soup all around!

If you're in Porto in the autumn, enjoy a rich and inviting bowl of *caldo de nabos*, a specialty of the nearby town of Gondomar. This creamy, robust turnip soup screams cozy with just enough bite

Left to right:

Bright *nabos* (turnips); *caldo verde*, the famed kale or collard greens soup of Minho.

to jump-start your circulation and just enough richness to feel loved. But don't be perturbed if the tubers don't sit well on your palate. Like cilantro, one can be genetically sensitive to turnips and other foods containing cyanoglucoside that release trace amounts of cyanide. If you've inherited two copies of the gene, you'll find these bulbous roots to be twice as bitter than normal.

Ana Cardoso comes from a long line of Gondomar farmers who've dedicated their lives to turnips. Much of what she sells at the market grows among her vast fields, which she tends to with her husband. Cameras seem to adore Ana, so if you think she looks familiar in your searches about Porto, you may have seen her in articles or YouTube videos shredding collard greens on her old creaky machine in the back of her stand.

"My customers come to me instead of supermarkets, because I won't shred up the stems with the leaves," says Ana, a dainty woman who possesses sufficient energy to fuel the entire city of Porto. "Doing it this way not only makes the kale more tender, but I get to feed my chickens with the leftover stems. It's how everyone did it in the past." Whether touting the quality of her crisp collard greens or sprucing up her attractive produce, no customer passes through without hearing a few salesy whispers from Ana.

Ana Cardoso shreds collard greens on her ancient, creaking machine.

To preserve shredded kale or collard greens in the fridge, leave the bag open. It will last longer!

In the age of mass production, it's incredible to know that the woman selling you collard greens is the very same woman who grew, picked, and shredded it by hand. No hidden agendas. No middleman. Just Ana. It goes beyond customer service; it's simple, genuine, and heartwarming. The fact that Ana and many of her peers grow their own fruits and vegetables is a major perk for patrons on the hunt for authentic, hard-to-procure items like the seasonal turnips from Gondomar that require an experienced hand to grow properly.

Left to right:

Headed cabbage abounds at the market; beautiful broccoli, bell peppers, and eggplant.

Years ago, these Gondomar farmers (and others from Northern towns like Barcelos, Pena Fiel, and Póvoa de Varzim) would pile their produce on horse drawn carriages to endure long, arduous trips to Bolhão. Others, like Albina da Silva, would "simply" hop on the train. One of the eldest vendors at the market, Albina recalls the number of crates she perpetually wheeled onto the platform. The number ranks in the triple digits. If you consider the uneven dirt and cobblestone streets, the weight of the load, and the enormity of her determination to either drag or carry her crates on top of her head from the station to the market at four in the morning, it's jaw-dropping to think about. That is, until you set eyes on her. With silver hair tied in a low-hanging bun, gently touching a blue and brown paisley kerchief she occasionally wraps around her head, Albina could organically be photoshopped into an early 1900s group photo of rural Portugal. She's the quintessential Portuguese grandmother—packed with Old World practicality and hardship stories.

Left to right:

Albina da Silva is the quintessential Portuguese grandmother, full of spunk and stories; *nabiça preta* **(turnip tops) are Maria Emília Santos's (Albina's daughter) favorite type of** *grelos.*

Like Albina, her daughter Maria Emília Santos has enough spit and fire to topple a sailor. Her opinions are overflowing and her filters are nonexistent. She's a woman of purpose accentuated by her tapered haircut and furrowed brow. But don't let her sourpuss temperament deter you, because under that hard shell lies an incredibly knowledgeable softie!

Check out her homegrown favorites including *grelos*, an all-encompassing term for varieties of turnip and spring greens. Harvested throughout the year, they're used in simple side dishes of boiled greens garnished with olive oil or sautéed in garlic. *Nabiça preta* (a type of turnip green) is Maria Emília's favorite. The Portuguese also use *grelos* to make a side dish called *esparregado*. Depending on what's in season, *grelos* might be substituted with *espinafres* (spinach) to create this veggie mousse. Either one is a stunning pairing with succulent roast meat—a Portuguese specialty.

Throw *grelos* into rice and the result is the popular pilaf called *arroz de grelos*. In the far corner of the market, under the grand staircase and behind the forest of ferns and technicolored orchids, you'll find a superb example of this rice dish—a Wednesday special on the homestyle menu at Café Da Gina. If you're looking for a strong pulse within the market, this is your place. Filled with a wide swath of

Grelos, some of which are marketed in the United States as either rapini or broccoli rabe, are a staple of Portuguese cuisine.

humanity eager for the upbeat, entertaining environment sparked by the owner's vivacious son, Nuno Fernandes, the café is rarely, if ever, empty. Hearty, warm, and filling, the bitter *grelos* give just enough of a mustardy bite and texture to complement the tame but rich tomato rice. It's the ideal dish to refuel your batteries before you embark on a second pass through the market.

In fact, these wholesome vegetable and rice combos are a mainstay in Portuguese cuisine (meat and seafood rice dishes are as well) because rice is surprisingly one of the country's largest crops. Portugal cultivates two main varieties of rice: *agulha* (long-grain rice) and Carolino. The former is a long-grain Indica rice that is commonly used as a side dish or for oven-baked rice dishes like the *arroz de pato* (duck rice). The latter is a native short-grain variety that's similar to the Italian Arborio rice. Low in amylose, it's ideal for creamy and *malandrinho* (saucy) rice dishes like *arroz de tomate* (tomato rice); *arroz de pimentos* (bell pepper rice); *arroz de feijão* (tomato rice with beans); *arroz de cenoura* (carrot rice)—the combinations are endless. Tidbit: the Portuguese consume about 35 pounds of rice per capita per year, compared with the approximate eight-pound European average, making them the top European rice lovers.

When asking for grelos *(turnip and spring greens), make sure that the "s" is pronounced loud and clear— otherwise you may be asking for a lady's love button.*

For the recovering Atkins dieters among you, consider Portuguese food your starch-friendly rehab cuisine. The Portuguese adoration of starch doesn't end with rice; it extends to magic flavored *batatas* (potatoes). They may look boring, but have one taste of Portuguese potatoes boiled and garnished with olive oil and sea salt and your knees will buckle in ecstasy. For double the starch love, it's common to find both rice and potatoes as side dishes on the same plate. But it's not always that simple. As with rice, the Portuguese have other uses for potatoes. For instance, the rustic *batata a murro* (punched potatoes) are boiled with their skins, then ruptured with a light punch and finished in the oven with olive oil–soaked octopus or cod. Peeled, thickly sliced, and inundated with fragrant broths, they're a flavor-absorbing delight in Portuguese stews. Homestyle restaurants indulge loyal patrons with extra sauce to savor those very last spuds sitting idly on their plates. Sigh—so, so good!

Left to right:

Garnished with rich olive oil, boiled potatoes in Portugal are a wholesome treat; young spuds are ideal for making *batata a murro*, roasted "punched" potatoes.

The Portuguese adore their piri-piri and jindungo, the chilies behind their fiery sauces.

Whether the star is rice or potatoes, there's one common ingredient that fires up Portuguese cuisine—piri-piri chilies. Discovered by the Portuguese in Mozambique, these long necklaces of bird's eye chilies are festively draped throughout the market, taunting bystanders with their ruby-esque glow. Through a veil of dangling garlic, Arminda and Laurinda Araújo whisper ancestral tips for transforming these tiny chilies into *molho picante* (hot sauce) at home.

"All you have to do is discard the little green stems, and then jam about 20 peppers into an empty honey jar. Fill half of it with olive oil, puree the ingredients with a hand blender, and finish with a few drizzles of olive oil to preserve," instructs Laurinda, adding that you can also spike it with a touch of whiskey, a common practice among barbeque restaurants. Though they don't grow their own crops, these savvy sisters source their produce from suppliers that they've built long-standing relationships with over the years, and who sell directly to them at the market.

"The garlic is picked during the feast of São João in June and lasts through the following São João. This type of [hardneck] garlic is stronger in flavor," Laurinda explains, holding a handful like a wedding bouquet. We're not surprised to see such an enamored grin on her face; garlic is after all one of the most used ingredients in Portuguese recipes, along with onions, scallions, and leeks. "When the garlic stems are green you can also cut those up for recipes like *favas com entrecosto*," or fava bean and rib stew.

Originally from Barcelos, the toothsome pair—one slender, one stout—were shipped off to Porto as young girls to work as maids. They've witnessed considerable changes to the city over the years and are now thrilled to see young families returning to the market.

Left to right:

Cebolas (onions) and *al ho* (garlic) make it into practically every dish in Portugal.

You'll get lots of sisterly love at Arminda (left) and Laurinda (right) Araújo's stand, where dried legumes, gigantic pumpkins, dangling garlic, and more burst in every direction.

In parts of rural Minho, it's traditional to eat *porta-de-loja* apples on Christmas Eve, baked and served in a bowl drizzled in Vinho Verde *tinto* (red sparkling wine) and sprinkles of sugar.

"A few years back that wasn't the case," says Arminda, "but now they like to pick up the products and ask questions." The sisters gleefully provide tips and custom service to their loyal clientele. On request, they peel and cube gourds, prepare string beans for soups, and explain what beans to use for which Portugese stew—and there are many (see Meat, page 138).

Like potbellied militiamen, gunnysacks erupting with red kidney beans for the *feijoada à Trans-montana*; white beans for *tripas à moda do Porto*; and garbanzos for *rancho à moda do Minho* perfectly line their stand. As these legumes are dried, they must undergo a rehydration process before being thrown into a dish. "It's so easy," the sisters say, "just rinse them in cold water and add them to a pot with enough water to cover them and let boil for five minutes. Once it boils, throw in cold water to shock the beans and quicken the cooking period, approximately 30 minutes." There are people who soak their beans in cold water overnight, but the sisters say they don't find it necessary. They also sell dried *tremoços* (lupini beans), which require a two-day soaking period to rehydrate their meaty interiors. When ready, they're boiled and then rested in cold water with salt for taste. These are common finds in Portuguese bars or taverns, alongside an ice-cold *cerveja* (beer)—but don't eat the skin! Gently pierce one side of the *tremoço* with your teeth and squeeze, allowing the bean to fly out of its shell and into your mouth. Tidbit: old-school Portuguese ingest a small lupini bean a day like a pill to help control diabetes.

Left to right:

From stews to salads, beans of all kinds are a beloved ingredient in Portugal; fat fava pods, an enticing halved pumpkin, bags of black-eyed peas, and fragrant onions.

To soothe a cough, the Portuguese slice a carrot thinly, add a couple of tablespoons of sugar (or honey) and water, cover, and let sit overnight to create *xarope de cenoura* (homemade syrup). The best part is that you get to eat the sweetened carrots, which in their raw state are chock-full o' vitamins.

Seek out *dióspiros* (persimmons) in autumn! These fleshy little color bombs can be found in two textures: jammy or crunchy. The second is ideal for nomadic sightseers.

At Mena Gabriel's stand, grab a fistful of sweet and succulent Moscatel grapes to curb your hunger and provoke a satiated smile. Harvested along the contoured hills of the Douro Valley and Trás-os-Montes, they're some of the very same grapes that produce the sumptuous dessert wine of Favaios. If you close your eyes, the flavor mirrors the wine so well that they seem indistinguishable.

Spring and summer, the market is blessed with a bounty of beautiful fruit from the Douro, including fat and chewy figs, juicy cherries, and some of the sweetest *melão* (honeydew) and *meloa* (cantaloupe) you'll ever taste. If you're cruising through the valley during warm months, chat up the apron-clad women on the side of the road. As streetwise and assertive as your neighborhood alley cat, these ladies specialize in only one product: fruit. Whether sumptuous cherries, peaches, or melons, there's always something sweet to devour in the Douro.

Because of Mena's slightly obsessive-compulsive tendency to preen, position, and polish each and every item at her stand, she's a master of visual art. Watch as she piles each fruit into a perfectly symmetrical pyramid of autumn color, or how she expertly pulps each persimmon into a silky fruit smoothie, provided freely to loyal customers and suppliers alike. Occasionally, suppliers will reciprocate with their own recipes. Mena's favorite is persimmon mousse, which she drizzles with Port wine or sprinkles with cinnamon. This give-and-take is the magic of the market—more than shopping, it's knowledge building.

Though fruity mousses (mango is a hit) are commonplace on dessert menus, fruit in itself is considered a sweet finale to any meal. At restaurants, patrons often opt for a slice of syrupy melon after their meal instead of a thick slice of almond tart (though it's equally amazing). And at home, families peel apples, pears, oranges, or whatever is in season before sipping on a creamy espresso. Ever try a baked apple soaked in Port wine and sprinkled with cinnamon sugar? No? You will now! You might also find a round of Terrincho sheep's cheese from Trás-os-Montes served at the same time, while dried or candied fruit (favorites include figs, dates, and raisins) are central to holiday dessert fare. As a matter of

Left to right:

In spring and summer, the market is perfumed with the sweet scent of strawberries. For a quick and refreshing dessert, simply add a dash of ruby Port wine and a sprinkle of sugar; like their Mediterranean kin, the Portuguese adore their dried fruits and nuts.

fact, raisins happen to be the celebratory fruit of the New Year. At the stroke of midnight, it's tradition to eat 12 raisins while making 12 wishes for each month of the New Year. Nuts are also integral to the Portuguese diet. There's even an entire autumn festival called São Martinho (Saint Martin) dedicated to *aguardente* (firewater) paired with boiled or roasted chestnuts. The intoxicating aroma of roasted chestnuts is commonplace throughout Porto as lone carts beckon children with a tasty after-school snack. Inside Bolhão, you can find a wide variety of dried fruits and nuts at Maria Teresa Ferreira's stand. Here olives rule, but she also carries a wide swath of other nibbles. Or pay a visit to the specialty shops along the exterior of the market, such as Casa Ramos, Casa Chinesa, Comer e Chorar por Mais, and A Pérola do Bolhão, which are rich with sweet and savory snacks.

Ermelinda Monteiro, a strawberry blonde (how appropriate), transforms a portion of her plump fruit into preserves: *doces* (jams), *geleias* (jellies), and *compotas* (compotes). Tourists go wild for them as they're easy to savor in your hotel or secret away in your luggage. But if you have to choose one, go for the tomato jam. When made well, the acidity will perfectly balance the savory sweet flavor, giving you a spreadable gift of the gods. A close second in popularity is the *marmelada* (marmalade), made from *marmelos* (quinces) and often paired with oozy Serra da Estrela cheese. Side by side with Ermelinda—and a vision of a preppy schoolgirl—is Maria Teixeira, who gets her gourds from her mother's farm in Pena Fiel. She also makes preserves, including the beloved *doce de chila*, crafted from a gourd similar in texture to spaghetti squash. Historically, it was one of the toughest gourds to prepare because the alloy steel knives of the day altered the taste of the final product—a chemical reaction said to be true of all Cucurbitas. Consequently, it required creative solutions to crack it open, such as a mallet or a swift throw to the ground. One way or another, there was no stopping the Portuguese from gutting the gourds to make their precious *chila* (a.k.a *gila*) sweets.

The most favored of the gourds is by far the green and yellow spotted *abóbora porqueira*. This gigantic specimen—capable of growing up to 77 pounds—weighs down dust-laden truck beds in late summer. The name *porqueira* derives from *porco* (pig), as they were originally intended to feed swine. Eventually, people crafted soups and jams out of them as well, but the name stuck! What comes closest to a Halloween pumpkin in Portugal is the *bolina* (a.k.a *menina*), the heroine behind the fluffy pumpkin fritters called *bolinhos de bolina*. Though most commonly served during the holidays drenched in a homemade syrup of sugar, Port wine, and cinnamon, you occasionally find them on dessert menus across the city. Some of the gourds at the market have even made it into Portuguese literary masterpieces. The late 19th-century writer Camilo Castelo Branco weaved into his writings mentions of the *calondro*, an elongated pale green gourd that, like the novelist, hails from the far North.

8.5% of *castanheiros* (chestnut trees) worldwide are found in Portugal, and 80% of Portugal's *castanha* (chestnut) production comes from villages in the district of Bragança.

Left to right:

Ermelinda Monteiro
and Maria Teixeira
transform some of their
vibrant fruit into jams,
jellies, and compotes.

What makes the fruits and vegetables in Portugal so special is how interconnected they are with the roots of the people. It's quite common to hear a Portuguese person in the city say "*eu vou à terra*," which translates to "going to my land." It doesn't matter which village someone is referring to, everyone understands that going back to your *terra* (also a word for soil) means you're visiting your origins, a place where you likely leave with a trunk overflowing with lemons, potatoes, nuts, olive oil—the bottom line is this: if they have it, you're going home with it!

And that's the beauty of Bolhão, too, where a majority of what you buy is freshly picked from area farms, orchards, vineyards, and in some cases, straight from city backyards. Shopping at these traditional markets is a return to home for the Portuguese—not merely figuratively, but literally.

Left to right:

The Portuguese love their lemons! When flu season hits, ask for a *carioca de limão* (hot water and lemon peel) to clear your sinuses and feel refreshed; for the Portuguese, shopping at Bolhão is a return to their roots; visit the market for the crispest produce daily; get a taste for homemade jams.

During the feast of São João, locals traditionally tapped each other on the head with alho-porro *(leeks) to ward off the evil eye. These days, most festivalgoers have traded in their leeks for colorful toy hammers.*

RECIPES AND RECOMMENDATIONS

Cantinho das Manas
RUA DA VESSADA, 39 4420 GONDOMAR
+351 224 646 242

If you adore treasure hunts, you'll love searching for this hidden gourmet oasis in Gondomar, nestled along the eastern border of Porto's metropolitan area. Ensconced in a web of *vivendas* (medium-size homes) and grassy fields is a cozy restaurant set within a stone house. Rich mahogany wood furniture and wrought iron chandeliers offset vibrant blue and white tiles and ornately framed mirrors. It's charming, medieval, and the perfect stage to watch Constança Cardoso create culinary masterpieces from the open kitchen. Bursting with emotion and power, her dishes are pure heart and soul. Try her award-winning *caldo de nabos,* a soup made with the local São Cosme turnips and other seasonal ingredients grown on her brother's farm. The São Cosme variety is key to the potent flavor of the soup, since it contains an extra dose of acidity. The turnips are pureed with potatoes, laced with lard, and garnished with pork and red beans, giving it a wholesome, rich flavor. It's the perfect dish to endure Porto's "tropical hurricanes" come winter.

CALDO DE NABOS
(Turnip Soup)

Yield: 8 to 9 servings
Time: 1 hour 45 minutes

2 pieces *ossinhos de suã* (pork neck
    or spine bone) with meat
½ cup dry red wine
Coarse salt, to taste
4 bay leaves
2 cups dry red kidney beans
2 large potatoes, halved
½ pound cured pork belly
3 tablespoons olive oil
½ cup cold water
4 medium turnips, thinly sliced
    and tops reserved

1. Combine the bones, wine, salt, and bay leaves in a bowl. Cover and let marinate for 12 to 24 hours in the refrigerator.

2. Discard the marinade and transfer the bones to a pot with the beans, potatoes, pork belly, and olive oil. Add just enough water to cover the ingredients. Set the pot over high heat and bring to a boil. Lower the heat to medium, add the cold water, and bring the mixture to a boil again. (This cooks the beans faster.) Repeat this process until the potatoes are tender, about 20 minutes. Taste and add salt as needed. It might not need any because the cured pork belly is salty.

3. Transfer the bones and potatoes to separate bowls and reserve the broth. Add the sliced turnips to the broth. Smash the potatoes with a fork and pull the meat from the bones. Return the potatoes and meat to the pot. Add the turnip tops to the broth.

4. Boil the soup for an additional 10 minutes and serve.

TIP: *Though a hotly debated topic among Portuguese grandmothers, some swear by soaking the beans overnight to cut cooking time exponentially.*

Restaurante Delicatum
RUA DO TAXA, 23, BRAGA
+351 253 619 584

Tucked into the backstreets of Braga, where only locals venture, you'll find Delicatum. Though wine is at its core, this is not your elitist restaurant demanding a degree in oenology. This is a cozy, homestyle bar run by a husband and wife team bubbling with an insatiable desire to entice your palate with both their exceptional wine list and their personalized *petiscos* (small bites). Try the pears poached in Port wine. This unassuming dish may seem basic, but its rustic appeal lies in its ability to pair with any season. Beyond a stellar dessert option, this succulent sweet treat also pairs well with grilled meat. Similar to an apple chutney, this dish is a fabulous balance to chargrilled flavors.

PÊRAS À VALE DO DOURO
(Pears Douro Valley Style)

Yield: 12 servings
Time: 1 hour

½ pound granulated sugar, divided
Peels of 2 lemons, divided
2 cinnamon sticks, divided
1 cup dry white wine
1 cup dry red wine
12 large, slighty underripe pears, peeled, halved lengthwise, and pitted
5 tablespoons white Port
5 tablespoons ruby Port

1. In a saucepan, combine half of the sugar, one lemon peel, one cinnamon stick, and the white wine. In another pan, add the remaining half of sugar, the second lemon peel and cinnamon stick, and the red wine. Bring both pans to a boil over medium heat.

2. Lower the heat to low, add 6 pears to each pan, and cook slowly until they're tender, about 30 minutes.

3. Put the white Port in the pan with the white wine and put the ruby Port in the pan with the red wine. Simmer for 10 to 15 minutes, until you have a syrup, but don't let it get too thick.

4. Place a half pear from each pan onto a plate, drizzling a spoonful of their respective syrups on top. Serve.

TIP: *Feeling extra sinful? Top the fruit with a dollop of vanilla bean ice cream and an extra drizzle of Port wine sauce.*

CHAPTER 3

FISH & SEAFOOD

"What struck me most in Portugal was the quality of its

fish and seafood. Wonderful and impressive. For me,

they are the best in the world."

—CHEF FERRAN ADRIÀ

❧

IT'S EARLY MORNING as vendors slowly shuffle into Bolhão in their vibrant street apparel smelling of perfume and espresso. Looking invigorated under freshly applied lipstick, they greet one another with hurried kisses as seagulls swoop and screech overhead. The air is crisp and cold, but pulsating with a sense of excitement and anticipation. Today is Saturday, one of the busiest days at the market. And in just a few hours, waves of tourists will pass through the long, decorated corridors, seeking out exotic stories and decadent flavors.

Amid a sea of stands, Bolhão's fish vendors steal the show with spurts of their sultry sales pitches. Called *pregãoes*, these enticing chants are an inheritance from the spunky and sensual Portuguese fishwife, an iconic and irresistible muse that has inspired music, sculptures, photographs, and movies since the early 19th century. The late Portuguese artist Rafael Bordalo Pinheiro was so bewitched by these fishwives (called a *vareira* in Porto, *varina* in Lisbon, and in general *peixeira*) that he created a statuette named *Ovarina* in tribute to her mystique, one in a series of ceramic figurines depicting caricatures of quotidian Portuguese life. With a heavy heart, these women followed their husbands from the fishing village of Ovar, just south of Porto, to the bustling big cities in search of work. The words *vareira* and *varina* are derivatives of "Ovarense," a person from Ovar.

Their allure is so enchanting, it's easy to imagine that these women are descendants of the Sirens in Greek mythology. Their magnetic musings, flowing skirts, and *canastras* (flat baskets) of fish propped

Portugal has the highest *peixe* (fish) consumption in the world. It takes only one bite to find out why!

precariously overhead cast a spell on the Portuguese collective imagination that has endured to this day. And though the spell of the *vareira* isn't deadly like that of the Sirens, it's nonetheless culturally powerful. Chances are you won't come across a hardcore *vareira* in Porto these days, but the image remains imprinted in the Portuguese memory.

With mouths as fresh as their fish, the vendors at Bolhão are the heiresses to the North's *vareira* legacy. The image of the fierce fishwife is so ingrained in the culture that it's stereotypical to call a rowdy woman a *peixeirona*. And if there's a ruckus, the derogative term *peixeirada* might be used, referencing the disruption a gaggle of rambunctious fishwives can cause. In fact, many of the fish vendors are proud of their trashy verbiage and consider it part of their persona. It's their way of *apimentar a vida*, to pepper life with spicy explicatives.

"Selling fish is good, but you can't forget to drop a curse word here and there, otherwise the ladies that come to shop would leave heartbroken," teases Maria Alice Ferreira, one of the most sought-after fish vendors at the market. She's in magazines, featured in cookbooks, and adored by tourists and photographers alike—everyone knows Maria Alice and her sidekick sister Ana Maria Ferreira. These two defy age. Though well into their 60s, they're as jubilant and lighthearted as the giggliest of teenagers.

Finishing each other's sentences, the sisters bicker and debate like an old couple and provide heaps of entertainment for onlookers. They embody gleeful grandmothers who spring to life at their neighborhood street festival. With the drop of a beat, they spin and sway under a blanket of flickering stars and multicolored ribbons, radiating sarcasm and survival. Their salt-and-pepper hair is short or wrapped in a bun, with little in the way of adornment or fuss. Because, quite honestly, they don't need it. Their sensuality and magnetism flows through their muscular hands, giving off an air of unquestionable professionalism and wickedly sharp intuition. Buried under layers of light sweaters, wool skirts, thick socks, and worn, flowery aprons, they're a testament to practicality and determination. Their joviality transports you to another time, to Porto during their youth and Bolhão at its best.

When selecting whole fresh fish make sure:
1. Eyes are bright and clear
2. Skin is taut and glistening
3. Belly is firm, not sunken
4. Gills are vibrant red
5. Smells salty and sweet, not rancid or fishy

Sisters Ana Maria (left) and
Maria Alice Ferreira (right)
attract hordes of journalists
and photographers with
their merry mood.

As the sun gently hides behind the clouds, masking the vibrant blue scales of the sardines, Maria Alice sits in comfortable repose on her throne, the place where her life has played 1,000 reels of fish stories. Arms casually crossed upon her voluptuous bosom, she takes a deep breath before letting her words trickle off her tongue and onto her lap, where a puddle of memories pools before us. There was a time, many decades ago, when she clambered onto an open-air cargo van, alongside her sisters and a handful of fellow vendors. On steamy, hot summer days, the women would revel in the gentle currents sweeping over the roof of the van as they made their way to the wharves of Matosinhos—a neighboring fishing village that is now a thriving suburb. Haggling for only the fattest, most succulent of fish, they would return to the van shortly thereafter with their loot in tow. With a sly grin, she says, "On one particular day, we got done early. So, with time to spare, we decided to stop over at Chaves where they make *iscas de bacalhau*, [a Northern variant of the ubiquitous *pataniscas de bacalhau*, codfish fritters]. We stuffed our faces and sang São João songs with the sizzling sun over our heads."

Consumed after it has been salted, dried, and soaked, *bacalhau* (cured cod) is undoubtedly the most emblematic fish in Portuguese cuisine. Since they landed on Newfoundland, the Portuguese have transformed fresh cod into planks of cured fish that are stacked or hung anywhere fish is sold. The village of Ílhavo (less than an hour south of Porto) pays homage to the *faina do bacalhau* (codfish toil) at its maritime museum with a permanent exhibit, *Rota do Bacalhau* (*Codfish Route*), tracing the Portuguese love affair with cured codfish to the Age of Discovery—a time when Portuguese explorers set out across the high sea to discover new land. *Bacalhau* naturally cured well, which kept it safe from spoiling on unrefrigerated ships, a common occurrence on long voyages.

Left to right:

Bacalhau (cured cod) is so integral to the culture's maritime history that the Portuguese call it their faithful friend; Albina Ferreira's stand is always packed with patrons.

Since then, Portugal has acquired an insatiable appetite for *bacalhau*, a fish they call *rei* (king) or *fiel amigo* (faithful friend). *Bacalhau* is also a favorite of the devout. Being a Roman Catholic country, the Portuguese traditionally turn to *bacalhau* recipes during religious observations to substitute meat dishes. On Christmas Eve, you might enjoy boiled cod, potatoes, kale, carrots, and eggs garnished with minced garlic, black pepper, parsley, and rich olive oil. From bar food favorites like *pastel de bacalhau* (codfish cakes) to the homestyle fare of *arroz de línguas de bacalhau* (brothy tomato rice with tender cod tongues, onion, garlic, white wine, and coriander), the Portuguese boast more than a thousand *bacalhau* recipes.

Though there is an abundance of delectable sea creatures in Portuguese waters, ironically, codfish isn't one of them. Since the 15th century, the Portuguese have fished (or imported) their faithful friend from foreign waters, such as Canada and Norway. In Newfoundland, the Portuguese fisherman connection is so strong that a statue of the Portuguese explorer Gaspar Corte-Real stands in front of the Confederation Building in St. John's, a donation from the Portuguese Fisheries Organization.

Portuguese fishermen, especially those from the islands of the Azores and Madeira, also dropped anchor in coastal towns in the United States, primarily in California and New England. Traces of this maritime past are especially evident in Provincetown, off the tip of Cape Cod, where by the late 19th

Left to right:

Pastéis de bacalhau (cured codfish cakes) are a prime example of Portugal's frittered finger foods; at the crack of dawn, fishermen in Matosinhos sort through their morning's catch.

The Portuguese love their crustaceans almost as much as they love their beer. Called an *imperial* in Lisbon, a *fino* in Porto, there's always a cold brew of Sagres or Super Bock on tap! But do check out the various Portuguese craft beers popping up across the country.

century more than half of the population, and its fishing fleet, were comprised of Portuguese fishermen and their families. In town today, you can attend Portuguese festivals as well as the annual maritime ritual of Blessing of the Fleet, a traditional observance from the old country that gathers the community to pray for safety at sea.

The Portuguese are distinctly aware of the dangers at sea, a key reason why they prize their seafood so highly. It's a cultural addiction, and a fiercely contagious one at that. Ferran Adrià, the renowned Spanish chef behind the legendary elBulli restaurant, is a huge fan of Portuguese fish and shellfish, claiming it's the best in the world. He's not alone. Due to Portugal's ideal coastal conditions, and the people's innate fishing talent, what lands on the table tastes of the sea! Combine this with the country's own magical pixie salt that heightens flavor, grilling techniques that opt for hot embers rather than flaming fires, and an all-around fish DNA that can be traced back to Lusitania (present-day Portugal), whose people produced top-notch *garum* (fermented fish sauce) for the Roman Empire, and it's easy to understand why Portugal is a mecca for world-class fish.

Mind you, their fame isn't restricted to cured cod or fresh fish; it extends to the art of manipulating and preserving some of the most coveted canned fish and seafood in the world. These Portuguese canned products sit regally on the shelves of top supermarkets. Once "poor man's food," Portugal's

Top left to bottom right:

Fishing boats sway softly at the Matosinhos docks as the morning fog slowly lifts; stone crab; prawns; shrimp.

canned seafood industry has completely turned around in the last decade, giving rise to top-quality brands (often canned by grandmothers) with funky retro labels that make for priceless souvenirs. The trend has also inspired a series of theme restaurants and specialty shops, such as Can the Can in Lisbon and Mercearia das Flores in Porto. Even wine shops, like The Bolhão Wine House inside the market, are working side by side with canneries to provide an entirely new pairing experience.

Despite their hardship at sea, fishermen have a wicked sense of humor—and the Portuguese are no different. These people are genius at telling jokes, belting out folklore tunes, and ripping up the dance floor. Sorrows at sea are a lesson to waste little time and live life to the fullest. It's not just about the work, it's about family and friends around jugs of wine and pots of comfort food like the *caldeirada de peixe* (fish stew), a recipe that originated with these fisherman families that made do with the honest ingredients they had on hand. Layers of potatoes, onions, tomatoes, and red bell peppers are topped with juicy chunks of fresh catch and a dash of wine, only to slow cook in a single pot to create pure, wholesome food. Today, this stew is a staple of Portuguese cuisine and common on restaurant menus.

As Ana Maria clips the fins off a silvery sea bass, a shrieky voice bounces off the counter: "It was more fun back then!" Maria Alice lets out a chuckle. "It sure was," she shouts over to the customer.

When boiling octopus, add a medium-size onion to the pot. If the onion is tender and you can poke a sharp knife to the core, the octopus is ready for eating!

Left to right:

Polvo assado no forno (roasted octopus) is a must-try dish; Portuguese canned fish and seafood are coveted by top supermarkets in the United States.

Opposite:

If you've always imagined octopus to be tough and chewy, try it in Portugal, where it's nice and buttery.

In between scaling and gutting fish, Ana Maria (pictured) and her sister Maria Alice don't shy away from a few sips of wine.

"There used to be this vendor that sang Fado really well, so she would sing songs the whole way back to the market. It was 10 or 12 of us in one van! What a riot!"

It's easy for Maria Alice to reminisce about Fado because singing is the cornerstone of a fish vendor's life, not only to create a festive atmosphere, but also as a means to overtake the fervent competition. Using a lilting yet commanding voice, the vendors woo passing customers with their sweet *pregão*. One might hear *"Amor, quer alguma coisinha?"* ("My love, want a little something?") or *"Há carapau e sardinha linda!*" ("There are beautiful mackerel and sardines!"). On crazy busy days, the fish vendors transform their lungs into megaphones, blaring these catchy pitches across the market. With their unwavering magnetism, you can imagine their effect as a means to grab your attention.

As jagged elbows and overstuffed bags careen into our sides, Maria Alice steps away from our conversation to help her sister attend to customer needs. Take a moment to watch her, because her uncanny skill to gut, clean, and butterfly an entire red snapper—while taking new orders, stealing glances in our direction, and occasionally looking behind her to watch her favorite Portuguese soap opera—is mind-boggling. She's a cross between the multiarmed Hindu goddess Kali and the Greek giant Argus, famous for his multiple sets of eyes. Except in this case, Maria Alice wields boning knives and fish guts, instead of a sword and a human head.

"Give me the chubby sardines," commands the customer. "Chubby like me," Maria Alice responds through a playful grin. The Portuguese are suckers for grilled sardines—the centerpiece of the country's saints feasts in June. In Porto specifically, come for São João (Saint John), a festival of firecrackers, floating lanterns, bustling parades, and traditional folklore music alongside top-notch bands. It's a time of year when fatty sardines and mackerel are grilled to perfection on every corner, terrace, and patio across the entire city. Your mission: grab a mug of wine or beer followed by a juicy sardine over a thick

In order for bustling fish houses to pack 'em in like canned sardines, fish is typically butterflied before being grilled over hot embers. The result: tender, flavorful meat wrapped in perfectly charred skin.

slice of *broa* and sigh in delight as you nibble off the meat. Flip the sardine and repeat. When finished, dive into the *broa*, which has soaked up every drip, dribble, and drop from the fish. It's a bib-worthy yet sensual experience.

Satisfied with her sardine sale, Maria Alice sits on her stool for a few seconds, folds her arms, and continues exactly where she left off: the *pregão*. She explains that each vendor individualizes her *pregão* depending on what's in stock that day. It's vocal bait! The *pregãoes* are tamer now than during the market's heyday, but they're just as meaningful and relevant as they were before. Often, these vendors reel you in with heartfelt promises of fish so fresh it's "alive!" They'll chant endearing versions of the fish names; the *carapau* turns into a *carapauzinho* and the *robalo* into a *robalinho*. Their fish is *lindo* (beautiful), and you are a "sweetie" and "good-looking." If you're in need of an ego boost, this is the place to be!

Consequently, if you're looking for a bargain, good luck, because haggling with these ladies is a sport. They're easygoing but will defend their fresh merchandise until their last breath. Having inherited a disciplined and prudent work ethic from their grandmothers and mothers before them, they're not eager to simply give in. They'll fight tooth and nail to get the best price.

"This isn't theater," Graça dos Santos emphatically bellows in a raspy voice that oozes Fado, the soulful music that captures so beautifully the bittersweetness of the Portuguese seafaring culture in several of its songs. In Praia do Titã, a Matosinhos beach, stands a haunting sculpture in tribute to the shipwreck of December 2, 1947, one of the worse ever in Portugal's history. The piece—*Tragédia do Mar* (*Tragedy at Sea*)—isn't of the 152 sailors swallowed up by the sea that day; it's of their desperate wives and children screaming from the sand as they realize their husbands, fathers, and brothers won't be returning home. On that day, 71 women were left widows and 100 children became fatherless. It's a heart-wrenching piece that captures the sense of melancholia planted in the Portuguese spirit. In part, it's a sentiment that resulted from a lifetime of maritime tragedies, a recurring theme in the musical genre of Fado, another word for "fate" in Portuguese.

As a passionate *fadista* herself, Graça's words weigh with an intensity that is reminiscent of the raw emotion in the soul music of Nina Simone, the American counterpart to Amália Rodrigues—the diva of Fado. Graça's eldest daughter has even inherited the bug; she's a Fado fanatic with fishwife DNA running through her veins.

Graça maintains intense eye contact while standing in the typical fishwife stance—shoulders straight, legs spread, hands on hips. Admittedly, it's intimidating, but the delicate pink shirt revealing a tad of cleavage beneath a thick gold necklace softens the effect. The look is topped with a pale yellow embroidered apron that matches her light, loose strands of hair. "Graçinha do Bolhão," as stated on her chalkboard, is sexy in a voluptuous, matronly "don't mess with me" sort of way. And although we agree that Bolhão is 100% real and not theater, classes in "fishwivery" to pick up the attitude and the almighty *pregão* sound incredibly appealing. Who couldn't use some tips on feminine badassery with Graça as a genuine mentor? She is, after all, the most flamboyant fish vendor in the market. She

Sardines are caught throughout the year, but the most succulent are harvested in late summer, when they're chubby, juicy, and flavorful.

When in season, the vendors at the market carry both the large *sardinha* (sardine) and *petinga* (small sardine).

Graça dos Santos
lures customers to
her stand with a raspy
Fado singing voice.

weaves spells and entrances like a snake charmer draped in intricately designed pieces of gold filigree jewelry—dangling earrings, rope chains, and gaudy pendants, which are a nod to key elements in the traditional *vareira* wardrobe. One of the most iconic of the fishwife costumes comes from Viana do Castelo in coastal Minho, where it's featured as a centerpiece of annual festivals in tribute to these ardent men and women of the sea.

Although these women are marked by their flair for fashion, their wrists and hands are always left unadorned as a sign of readiness to work, a tie to years of taking over the helm of their households as the men went off to sea. When they returned home from their voyages, the women hardly interrupted their reign, as their husbands longed for repose. And when tragedies knocked on their doors, they morphed (and still do) into fierce matriarchs ready to fight for their family's survival. Long before women's rights gained momentum in Portugal, they had been a symbol of fortitude, a trait still alive and kicking inside the market.

The essence of these fish vendors is fundamental to a traditional market like Bolhão. Had city officials supported this heritage, rather than banning families from passing down their stands through the generations, Graça's daughter might see a future in taking over the business. The hope is that a new Bolhão can restore the interest in maintaining a traditional market, a worthwhile investment in a city like Porto where tourism is booming.

And don't think that just because they're old school these vendors don't embrace change. On the contrary, they know damn well what it's like to have to adapt to various difficult situations, and have continually done so over the years. They understand and encourage Bolhão to change as long as there's respect for its heritage as a traditional market. Many of them advocate organizing events at the market to attract a new crowd. Fado nights for instance, suggests Graça. She already knows two *fadistas* that would be interested. Wink.

Itching to haggle at Bolhão? Unless you're a regular this might be out of your league. But rumor has it that if you buy larger amounts, even one extra shrimp, the price might drop.

When choosing a plank of bacalhau, *make sure it's not only the whitest of the bunch, but also the thickest in the middle.*

The vast increase and impact from tourism within the market has been incredibly motivational. Many of the vendors have expressed an interest in expanding their businesses, but with the market's future in limbo their requests have remained unmet by market officials.

"How many times have I been here by myself frying up sardines to eat with a piece of *broa* and a glass of wine, and when tourists saunter by I share a fried sardine with them. I don't sell it, I give it away. This is how I would like it to be. If they would only let me put a table next to my stand for people to sit," Graça says, shrugging her shoulders in annoyance. "Who wants more awful shopping malls? Look at Bom Sucesso [another market], it's all gourmet—to heck with that! Bolhão is centenary, there are folks with three generations in here like me. My mother carried me in her womb in Bolhão. I was born here, I want to die here."

Maria Natalina Lapa has longed to move to a larger space, one that would allow her to whip up some *petiscos* (small bites) like *rissóis de camarão* (shrimp turnovers) to serve with a glass of wine. What we see in Maria Natalina is culinary television show material. By her slender figure, firm skin, and sandy cropped hair, you wouldn't know that Maria Natalina is nearing 70. In her makeshift kitchen behind the counter, she stirs a wooden spoon inside a beat-up pot from where tantalizing scents snake around our senses. We detect *lulas* (squid). Maria Natalina returns from her pot and confirms our suspicions that it's *caldeirada de lulas* (squid stew), then tells us about the deboned and butterflied sardines laid out on her display.

Working with fish is so intuitive that vendors can do it blindfolded.

"The other day, I saw a television chef make a *robalo* (sea bass) soup and he wasted so much of the fish because he didn't know how to properly debone it," she said. "I thought to myself, what a waste it is for me not to have the proper exposure at the market." Bingo, we knew it—a natural-born television star.

Maria Natalina continues, unaware of the visions we have for her in our zealous minds. "There are people who won't eat fish because of the bones, but if they saw this, they would realize they could take their fish home without one single bone in it." Tourists love to watch her work, reveling in her skill and efficiency. "They value and appreciate the fish and ask questions. They say I'm a master; they even applaud me." She lets out a shy giggle. "They stay here observing me as if I'm some kind of monument."

What Maria Natalina may not realize is that she should be treated like a precious monument—not one made of steel or stone, but of stories and traditions that can be passed on to new generations. At the heart of it, that's what these women's lamentations (and ours) are all about. It's not about a sense of entitlement, it's a desire to preserve what's real and an instinct to fight for survival. This reminds us that the human heritage of Bolhão should be as valued as the architectural heritage of the market's beautiful structure, currently protected as a public interest monument.

Graça and Maria Natalina are not alone either. Nearly all of the vendors we spoke to have dreams of expanding and developing new ideas, all while sharing the memories and know-how from previous generations. They're in no way obsolete. In fact, we need more competent people like them that understand what they're selling in and out of the market.

In Portugal, you can order a large *cabeça de peixe* (fish head) as your meal. After all, it's the tastiest part!

It's not all heads and tails at the market—you can ask to have your fish filleted and deboned.

The vendors inside Bolhão have always strived to provide a customized and competent service that sets each one apart from their competitors. Unlike supermarket employees, they don't have set salaries, so they must work hard to please customers. "I don't want to disrespect anyone, but it has happened to me at a local supermarket," says Albina Ferreira. "As a matter of fact, the girl who took care of me knew me from Bolhão. They told her to clean and prep a monkfish, and she didn't even know from which end to pick up the fish. From outside the counter, I tried to give her some pointers, but wasn't allowed to go back there, otherwise I would have stepped up and done it for her."

You can't compare. Bolhão's fish vendors are a treasure trove of knowledge and old-school tricks. Maria Alice and Ana Maria, for instance, pack up their fish with a large kale leaf. The kale helps keep the fish cool. "We had one customer that would come here to buy fish for her employer, and when the boss didn't see a kale leaf with the fish, she would say to her that she didn't go to the same fish vendor that day," says Maria Alice. "Our aunt used to do this, and it works. It preserves the fish in both cool and warm temperatures."

If you speak to Ermelinda Lopes—who differentiates herself and fellow third-generation vendors as the "descendants"—you'll learn all sorts of fascinating Bolhão trivia. From fresh fish to frozen seafood, Ermelinda has covered the gamut. As she leans in over the counter replete with codfish loins and gigantic octopus tentacles, her ash-blonde hair cascades over her shoulders, exposing the golden cobra-ribbed rim of her glasses. She's sweet but serious, with countless stories that flow without borders.

Adjusting her bleached apron, she shares the backstory to her grandmother's nickname while tapping her hand gently on her lap. To avoid massive confusion among the vendors at the Matosinhos fish auction, the fishermen would bestow *calões* (nicknames) to each one. Her grandmother, who raised her after her mother passed away, was called Palmira Alta. Using her name, Palmira, as fodder, the men

Don't be afraid of your neighborhood percebes (gooseneck barnacles). Despite their dinosaur-esque appearance, they're some of the most refreshing and delicious crustaceans you'll ever enjoy.

Ermelinda Lopes is one
of the "descendants"
of the market.

teased their way to the Portuguese word for palm tree, *palmeira*. Then taking her height, extraordinarily tall (like grandmother like granddaughter), they leapt to *alta*. The name wasn't meant in a derogatory or insulting manner. Much like your family or close friends might give you a nickname based on a shared moment, *calões* helped to nurture affection and friendship.

Stationed in the largest stand at one end of the market, Ermelinda has a wide view of who enters and leaves Bolhão. With her fierce sense of independence and authoritarian demeanor, she's unofficially become the market pit bull.

"In my grandmother's time, we had two supervisors, now we just have one," she says. "We also had about six security guards along with police. Now, if someone wants to rob and hurt us, we have to defend ourselves." She points to a bat that's hanging on the wall behind her and adds, "the reason that's hanging up there."

That same bullheaded determination extends well beyond the walls of Bolhão. Across the river from Porto lies the laid-back village of Afurada (home to generations of fisherman families), where festive dories hand-painted with bold stripes and tagged with quirky names, such as *Menino do Douro* (*Boy of the Douro*), litter the coastline. As the breeze carries mouthwatering aromas of salt and sardines grilling over hot coals, a burgundy suede cap peeks over a mound of orange nets, where a *pescador* (fisherman) sits serenely mending and patching torn mesh to the sound of the sea. The *assador* (grill master)—oftentimes the restaurant owner—stands terrace-side with worn tongs and agile wrists to flip grill baskets filled with sardines. As he butterflies an entire fish in one stroke, his wife conducts a culinary orchestra among kitchen staff, hungry patrons, and street merchants, who occasionally weave through tables in hopes of getting one good sale. She doubles as a waitress and triples as a baby entertainer, the kind of woman that cleverly stashes dinosaurs in her silverware drawer to keep your toddler smiling. Her superb multitasking is inherited from a culture that demands flexibility, strength, and leadership.

This is the same warmth you'll find in Bolhão. Despite its rawness, the market is a place where time is etched on every tile and every wrinkle. There's a sense of community here—a true feeling of home. It feels protected from malevolent intentions and nefarious deeds, giving rise to hope. These women, despite broken promises and divisions, remain resilient and welcoming. They look out for one another, as they've always done. Even the cats are well nurtured with leftover scraps of fresh catch.

There's a genuine respect for each and every role within the market, a loving web of interconnectedness. For instance, helping restaurants with their chores might be a way of thanking them for their business. So, don't be surprised to find a fish vendor peeling potatoes for your next meal. It's an ebb and flow that shows community and camaraderie.

On a lazy autumn afternoon, a request for *robalo* echoes across the market as eyes glance skyward in search of the source. Alert and ready for action, Sara Araújo grabs a medium-size silvery sea bass from her ice display, darts over to the communal water pump for a quick splash, then plops it on a steel

Clockwise from left:

The *assador* (grill master) churning out delectable fish at O Lusitano in Matosinhos; colorful dories; daily specials at Taberna de São Pedro at Afurada; a heavenly meal of Portuguese grilled fish.

tray and hand delivers it to Cafetaria Pintainho (run by a husband and wife duo, José and Paula Silva, who proudly serve only homemade fries, a luxury in the era of frozen spuds). Not a minute later, Sara's big black galoshes are on the move again, but this time it's to answer a call for an *atum* (tuna) steak.

In her 40s, Sara is one of the youngest fish vendors at the market, but don't let her scrawniness and wild ebony tresses fool you—she's hardcore. When her mother decided to stay at the wharves in Matosinhos and dedicate herself to the fish auctions 25 years ago, Sara took over at Bolhão. "There isn't anybody who knows more about fish than we do. I've even had to fight off a live conger! I had to whack it over the head with a stick, because the thing just didn't want to die!"

This sense of community also came in handy when raising children at the market. Many of today's vendors are a product of that communal child-rearing, which taught them not only to care for themselves but for those around them. Everyone chipped in—which might explain the sweet empathy that organically pours out of every gesture and gentle word.

"Our mothers needed to take care of their customers, so we had to look after one another. Bolhão was all for one and one for all," says Zaida Ferreira Silva, who's listening to a daytime television interview with love ballad singer Tony Carreira, a heartthrob for many middle-aged Portuguese women. As Zaida confides that she has tickets for his show in Lisbon, her grin widens. His personal life has been

A little spray of lemon juice adds a touch of fresh acidity to your perfectly grilled fish.

Sara Araújo may be petite, but she's all might while carrying a haul of fish; below, she preps gigantic squid for a customer.

all over Portuguese entertainment news since the announcement of his impending divorce, but he promised fans that he still wants to stay friends with his wife. Well played, Tony! Well played.

Flaunting a boyish hairdo that complements her youthful round face, Zaida speaks in a *bagaço* tone; it's what the Portuguese call a moonshine voice. In a raspy whisper she discreetly recounts her bittersweet memories to us. Zaida was raised in Bolhão and recalls playing with Ermelinda and some of the other descendants inside the market's warehouses. For these women, Bolhão wasn't simply a market, it was their home.

"Ermelinda was raised with me. That other one down there, Graça, was too. Conceição, the tall blonde, is also from my time. We played a lot," says Albina, whose nickname growing up was Joaninha (Ladybug) because she was tiny (still is) and fluttered about at the sound of a tune. "We would go inside the storage area to sing and dance. We played hopscotch, jump rope—all of those games you hardly see kids playing these days," she says. "Back then, there were so many people in Bolhão that we could hardly move, so our mothers would shove us in the storage areas, our private playgrounds."

But not all of the children in Bolhão were there with their mothers; some were there as full-fledged employees. That was the case of Rosa Maria Bispo Castro, a dainty vendor that rocks a pixie haircut and defines her cattish eyes in black liner. Compared to everyone else, she looks punk. She was so short when she started working at the market that her employer had to place her on top of a box so that she could reach the counter. Rosa Maria started working at Bolhão when she was 12 during school vacation, and vividly recalls those times.

If you're dying to sink your teeth into a blood sucking tube demon, also known as a lampreia *(lamprey), come in spring during their spawning season. These alienish freshwater fish are stewed in their own blood and served over rice. Therapy not included.*

Zaida Ferreira Silva
holds up a handful of
frozen *iscas de bacalhau*
(fried codfish pockets).

Maria da Conceição dos
Santos Soares always has
meaty salmon on offer.

Rosa Maria Bispo Castro started so young at the market that her boss propped her up on a box to reach the counter.

To remove salt and rehydrate *bacalhau*, place the fillet in ice-cold water, skin side up, for three days. Change the water once in the morning and once at night.

"I remember it as if it were today," says Rosa Maria. "On Fridays and Saturdays, it was a madhouse. I handled deliveries for my boss, and with a box of orders atop my head, I maneuvered through the market's mob saying 'excuse me, excuse me' the whole way. Sometimes, I had no choice but to pull on people's clothes so they would notice me. My boss would order me to run as fast as I could on errands to get them done quicker. But there was another vendor, Senhora [Mrs.] Fernanda, who had a daughter my age and felt sorry for me. Once she called me over and said 'on the way there, you walk slowly. On the way back, you run as fast as you can because you're light as a feather.' I took her advice. You should have seen how fast I would run on the way back. Even today, I run really fast!"

Rosa Maria's boss would often suggest that if she was well behaved the stand would eventually be hers. In time, she did open her own stand in Bolhão, though different from the original. That changed when a fire broke out in 2012 after a short circuit at one of the fish stands on the ground level. There were no injuries, but a series of stands were terribly damaged, including Rosa Maria's. But as fate would have it, she returned to her childhood stand, a place she both owns and calls home today. Giggling, she quips, "I guess I did behave after all." Thanks to her fellow vendors, who volunteered their time and lent the necessary equipment, Rosa Maria was settled into her new stand within days.

"The people from Porto are extremely warmhearted," says Sara. "If you need help, they lend a hand. If you don't know the way, they'll take you there. Helping others is already in the blood." Multiply this deep-hearted generosity by nearly 100 eager vendors, and you have a concentration of kindness in Bolhão, where customers leave with more than bags full of fish and fruit.

"Customers ask me 'Senhora Sara, do I fry my sardines in a dusting of wheat or corn flour?' I tell them corn flour, because it's smoother." Shaking her head from side to side, Sara smiles proudly, "You just can't beat these wisdoms."

Sara Araújo comes from a
full-fledged Matosinhos
fisherman family.

RECIPES AND RECOMMENDATIONS

O Gaveto

R. ROBERTO IVENS 826, MATOSINHOS
+351 229 378 796

A quick taxi ride from downtown (Baixa) Porto along the Douro River will bring you to the seaside town of Matosinhos, home to some of the best fish and seafood restaurants in the world. Top among them is O Gaveto, which has been in the trusted hands of Manuel Faria Pinheiro da Silva and his three children (José Manuel, João Carlos, and Isabel Cristina Fonseca da Silva) for more than three decades. Top winemakers from across the region have made this their lunch spot for decades, in part because of its exceptional wine list, but also because of its unbelievable seafood. Choose your catch from the numerous tanks greeting you at the door or revel in the mounds of locally caught gooseneck barnacles, mussels, and sweet orange shrimp. The *sapateira recheada* (stuffed stone crab) is by far one of our favorites. Steamed, dissected, and elegantly served on an ornate tray alongside thin toast, there's nothing as delectable, creamy, or gluttonous as that first bite!

SAPATEIRA RECHEADA
(Stuffed Stone Crab)

Yield: 4 servings
Time: 30 minutes

20 cups water (that's 1 gallon + 4 cups)
3½ cups coarse salt
1 (2–3 pound) live stone crab
1 *broa de milho* (cornmeal bread), crust removed
  and chopped
1 small yellow onion, chopped
¼ cup store-bought pickled cauliflower florets
1 egg, hard-boiled, peeled, and grated
1 tablespoon flat-leaf parsley
4 tablespoons lager beer
4 tablespoons tawny Port wine
1 tablespoon mayonnaise
Piri-piri hot sauce, to taste
Toast, for serving

1. Combine the water and salt in a large pot set over medium-high heat and bring to a boil. Add the crab and cook, uncovered, for 18 minutes.

2. Remove the crab from the pot and run it under cold water. Break off and reserve the claws and open the shell (see Tip), making sure not to lose any of the liquid inside it. Pour the liquid from the shell into a bowl.

3. Add the chopped *broa de milho*, onion, pickled cauliflower, egg, parsley, beer, wine, mayonnaise, and piri-piri. Mix with a fork and pour back into the crab shell.

4. Transfer the shell to a serving plate, decorate with the claws, and serve with toast.

TIP: *To use the shell as a bowl, position the crab on your left palm (ribbed side up), and with your right middle fingers shoved into the mouth of the crustacean, pull back as if you're opening a can of tuna.*

O Paparico

RUA DE COSTA CABRAL 2343, PORTO

+351 225 400 548

O Paparico is nestled in the suburban outskirts of Porto. If you aren't privy to its location and elusive entry, you could easily pass it by as a watering hole filled with neighborhood residents. But one peek inside and you're absolutely clear that you've entered a parallel dimension filled with glowing candelabras, cozy wooden ceilings, and ridiculously friendly staff. The concept is centered on sharing to nurture opportunities where patrons can mutually experience a moment. Every dish is portioned for at least two people—the monkfish rice, loaded with shrimp and chunks of luxurious fish in a savory tomato broth, is a must try. It's a lovely way to step away from our individual experience to something more intimate and personal.

ARROZ DE TAMBORIL
(Monkfish Rice)

Yield: 2 servings
Time: 45 minutes

5 cups Caldo (recipe follows)

¼ cup + 1 tablespoon olive oil, any type, divided

½ cup chopped yellow onion

½ cup chopped red bell pepper

1 bay leaf

1 clove garlic, minced

½ cup uncooked Carolino or Arborio rice

Salt, to taste

½ cup Alvarinho white wine

1 medium tomato, diced

1 pound monkfish

¼ pound raw fresh shrimp, cut into ½-inch cubes

Tabasco, to taste

Fresh flat-leaf parsley, to taste

1. Place the Caldo in a pot and bring it to a simmer. This should be simmering, not boiling, the whole time, so you may need to adjust the heat to keep it there.

2. In a pan, heat ¼ cup of the olive oil over medium heat until the first sign of bubbling. Add the onion, bell pepper, and bay leaf. Cook, stirring occasionally, until the onion is golden. Add the garlic and cook, stirring, for a few seconds.

3. Add the rice and cook until it is golden. Add the salt and wine, and, stirring constantly, the tomato. Add a ladleful of the simmering broth and, stirring constantly, allow it to absorb into the rice. Keep adding the simmering broth, one ladle at a time and stirring, allowing the broth to completely absorb before adding another.

4. When the rice is tender but not soft, add the monkfish. Cook for 5 minutes.

5. In the meantime, in a separate pan, heat the remaining 1 tablespoon of oil over medium heat until it shimmers. Add the shrimp and cook, stirring frequently, for about 2 minutes, or until the shrimp are cooked through.

6. Season with a dash of Tabasco and top with the shrimp and chopped parsley.

TIP: *Don't have an Alvarinho? Don't worry, any white wine with good acidity will do. However, we do highly recommend getting your hands on an Alvarinho from the Vinho Verde to sip while you cook.*

CALDO
(Broth)

Yield: About 5 cups
Time: 1 hour 30 minutes

1 tablespoon vegetable oil
½ pound monkfish bones
¼ cup olive oil
1 bay leaf
1 teaspoon ground coriander
1 teaspoon freshly ground black
    pepper
⅓ cup chopped yellow onion
2 shrimp heads
2 cloves garlic
1 teaspoon paprika
3 ounces brandy
½ cup Alvarinho white wine
⅓ cup coarsely chopped leeks
¼ cup coarsely chopped carrots
½ cup coarsely chopped red bell
    pepper
1 teaspoon coarsely chopped
    Scotch bonnet chile
2 medium tomatoes, diced
4 cups water
Flat-leaf parsley, to taste

1. Preheat the oven to 350°F.

2. Grease a baking dish with the vegetable oil. Add the bones and roast for about 30 minutes, or until they are caramelized. Be sure to vigorously shake the tray at least twice during the roasting time so that the bones on the top move to the bottom. This will help the caramelization process.

3. In a saucepan, add the olive oil, bay leaf, coriander, and black pepper. Warm over medium-low heat for 1 to 2 minutes, then add the onion and shrimp heads. Cook, stirring occasionally, until the onion is golden.

4. When the bones are ready, add them to the saucepan along with the garlic and paprika. Stir in the brandy and wine, cooking until they evaporate. Add the leeks, carrots, red bell pepper, and bonnet pepper. Simmer for a few minutes.

5. Add the tomatoes and simmer for 2 minutes. Add the water, cover, and bring to a boil over medium-high heat. Lower the heat to medium low and simmer for 1 hour.

6. Remove from the heat, garnish with parsley, and serve.

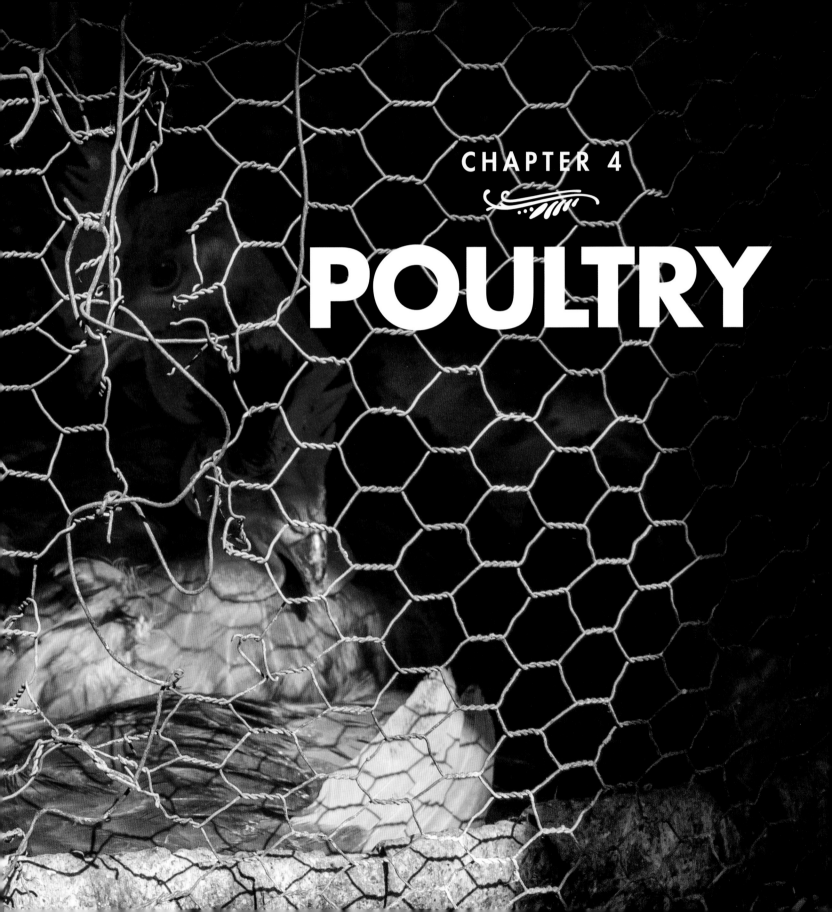

CHAPTER 4

POULTRY

"If you've never had quail, you have to try it. It's like chicken's sexy, chic cousin—way more savory and juicy, but not as intense as other game."

—CHEF GEORGE MENDES

AFTER WEEKS OF rain and mist, a crisp and bright Friday morning sky canopies life inside the market. Soaking up the soothing rays that seep into their wire mesh cages, the chickens at Lucinda Leite's stand couldn't be more appreciative. A relic of a time when the market fluttered with live birds of all kinds, Lucinda's coops are the purest link to the identity and history of Bolhão. With fiery squawks that echo deep into the produce and bread stands, these birds' sunrise song feels vibrant, energetic, and pulsing with life.

Yet in many cities around the globe, our only interaction with chicken is when it's perfectly dissected and shrink-wrapped for convenience. Over the years, even this has become too inconvenient, giving rise to boneless, skinless chicken that bears no resemblance to its former self. This kind of false comfort comes at a cost. Not only does it compromise taste—discarding the chance to enjoy succulent dark meat and crispy charred skin—but it dismisses the philosophical conversation about the food in front of us. It stifles questions about the conditions in which the animal is being raised, what it's fed, how it's slaughtered, and how it's prepared for consumption. It's an out of sight, out of mind mentality that often leads to a lack of critical thinking and irresponsible eating, which as we all know is a major contributor to modern-day diseases. What's the cure? Perhaps we can start by generating respect for markets like Bolhão.

At Bolhão, there's still an effort to preserve the connection between the origins of food and the

For a colorful souvenir, grab a Galo de Barcelos, the emblematic rooster of Portugal.

Opposite:

Though Lucinda Leite is no spring chicken, she's full of life!

people who eat it. Here, the chicken still bocks and has feathers, and its freshly butchered meat boasts smooth, unfettered feet and regal, red combs. Nothing in Bolhão is sugarcoated. There's no desire or need to hide life. There's value to buying a live chicken, whose fresh blood enriches the aromatic rice dish of *arroz de cabidela*, and whose offal and feet metamorphose into *pipis*, a *petisco* (small bite) of stewed chicken gizzards, hearts, liver, and feet in a savory gravy of onions, garlic, tomatoes, spices, herbs, and a dash of piri-piri (see Fruits & Vegetables on page 58). There's comfort in knowing that the woman selling you that chicken not only raised and nurtured it but killed it herself. These vendors are more than salespeople; they're agents of sustainability.

And no other vendor at the market embodies this spirit as profoundly as Lucinda, who stocks her stand with chicken, duck, turkey, pheasant, partridge, quail, and more. She travels north of Porto to the agricultural fairs of Ponte de Lima and Barcelos to acquire any poultry that she doesn't raise on her property. The latter is home to Portugal's emblematic rooster, Galo de Barcelos.

As legend has it, a Galician pilgrim was falsely accused of stealing silver while passing through the medieval city of Barcelos. Sentenced to death, the man begged to meet the judge who had determined his fate. "It's as certain that I am innocent as it is certain that this rooster will crow when they hang me," the man declared while pointing to a rooster ready to eat on the dinner table. Seconds before the pilgrim was to hang, the dead rooster crowed. In desperation, the judge flew down to the gallows to release the man only to find him saved by a loose knot. The story speaks to the Portuguese belief in integrity, honesty, trust, and honor, not to mention delicious poultry!

On her property in Vila Nova de Gaia, Lucinda raises an impressive array of birds, including a breed of Australianas (Australian hens), which are sought after for their dark meat. The eggs were gifted to her more than 20 years ago, and she has been raising the chickens ever since. She also sells pet birds, such as *pombas de leque* (fantail pigeons) and racing pigeons (the birds are trained to fly a measured distance until they return home). Like Lucinda, many Portuguese traditionally set aside a sliver of land for vegetable gardens and chicken coops, and that's where Lucinda's *garnizas* (bantam hens) come into play. Famous for their motivational brooding techniques, customers use these birds to speed along the hatching process.

When buying a live chicken or turkey—What? Doesn't everybody?—make sure its feet are smooth and the crest bright red. Rough feet signal old age and a dull crest poor health.

For the butcher savvy among you, Lucinda will happily sell the chickens straight out of the cage and into a poultry-friendly box to cart home. If you're a city dweller, or renting an Airbnb on your vacation, you may not feel "comfortable" performing a Friday evening chicken sacrifice while sipping on your white Port aperitif. So for you, choose a *caseiro* (homebred) bird on the spot and let Lucinda handle the rest, including the accoutrements. Unlike the preservative-laden chicken blood from the slaughterhouse, the blood from Lucinda's chickens is organic, refreshed with a few spoonfuls of vinegar to prevent coagulation, and good for about two weeks when kept cold. Though none of this is particularly "above the board," Lucinda is doing her very best to provide top-quality meat while the market ebbs and flows into a new design.

This rebellious, entrepreneurial spirit, expressed in her mischievous smile and sassy hip sway, isn't new to Lucinda. From the wee age of five, she tag teamed with her mother to ruffle a few feathers. Historically, vendors were required to pay a fee at the city border for every bird put on display; *borrachos* (baby pigeons) were taxed the highest. Fees varied, but the vendors' attitudes were the same—a common desire to save money. In this case, Lucinda would stash her fowl friends under a floor-length black shawl that draped loosely around her tiny frame, so that when the taxman called, she would make herself invisible. "While the officers counted my mother's chickens," Lucinda says, "I would quietly slip away with the hidden birds to a house in the distance to wait for her."

A Portuguese pregnancy myth promises lots of breast milk if moms down bowl after bowl of canja *(chicken soup).*

When hearing this story, you have to wonder what it feels like to have a baby pigeon strapped to your body. And how does one silence a pigeon? Are there age-old pigeon stifling techniques? And how do you repeat your fiendish escapade for the umpteenth time?

"They're just a month or two old," Lucinda laughs, "so even when I had a half dozen or more huddled under my shawl, they just sat quietly and mostly relaxed." Lucinda's chuckles are heartfelt and contagious. She beams with pride and overflows with love for her mother's mischief—until an internal dam breaks open. Tears well up, shoulders cave in, and her body gives way to *saudades*—a profound sense of loss and longing.

As cats yowl in the distance and blue shadows move across fissured concrete, Lucinda quickly soothes her own grief. Her contoured and lined fingers smooth away her tears. Smiling, we focus the conversation on the vibrancy of her memories, on her bravery and humor. Lucinda's smile returns. There's a heartbeat to Lucinda, a woman who slaughters to survive and to stay intimately connected to her past and principles.

Lucinda's unbending vigor is inspiring. Though well into her 80s, she has the spirit of a 20-year-old. Despite her unwavering passion and determination, her family is itching for her to retire, if only to care for her fragile spine. "I have a lot of strength," she boasts while wiping her hands on her checkered apron. "I'm able to do everything here by myself." Her smile widens with moxie galore. "What else can I tell you—I'm not leaving."

That's certainly the wish of her loyal customers, who turn to Lucinda for quality birds. The Portuguese appreciate a wide variety of poultry. It takes considerably less land, food, and manpower to raise birds than it does other livestock, which is why the regular use of poultry in meals is appealing to everyone. However, the ubiquity and affordability of chicken undoubtedly makes it the bird that reigns the Portuguese coop—but don't tell the *pato* (duck) or *codorniz* (quail) this! These fine feathered friends fall slightly behind in popularity, trailed only by the *peru* (turkey), which graces the occasional holiday table, gets *guisado* (braised), or shows up as cutlets for hungry children. Seasonally, you can also find game birds such as partridge and pheasant as well as the occasional goose and pigeon on the menu.

Chicken is an interesting case study of Portugal's fusion cuisine. Traditional chicken recipes, such as rustic roasts doused in garlic, herb, and olive oil marinades, are clear representations of the country's Mediterranean roots. Yet there are *quiabo* (okra) and *caril* (curry) flavors that the Portuguese picked up from their former colonies in Africa and Asia.

The Portuguese equally left their mark in every port of call, as evidenced in India's *vindaloo*, derived from the Portuguese words for *vinho* (wine) and *alho* (garlic). *Vindaloo* is a variant of *vinha d'alhos*, a pickling marinade the Portuguese use to tenderize meat. This intense marinade is so ingrained in the culture that any die-hard Portuguese can immediately conjure up that tangy, slightly spicy aroma lingering in their grandmother's fridge. Though it varies somewhat by region, the base of the marinade consists of garlic, pepper, paprika, wine, and fresh parsley or cilantro. Bay leaves, piri-piri, and *massa de*

It's believed that chicken soup is called *canja* and not *sopa* because of Portugal's ties to China, where it's called *congee* and is made with rice like certain Portuguese versions.

Hints of Portugal's vast global empire can be traced through the Portuguese's use of African and Asian spices.

pimentão (red bell pepper paste, see Fruits & Vegetables on page 166) are also used, alongside vinegar or lemon juice for extra zing. Add chicken and chilies, and you get one of India's most beloved curry dishes—chicken *vindaloo*.

These cosmopolitan flavors surfaced in Lisbon during the Age of Discovery. However, it was during the postcolonial era—when Lisbon became home to vibrant multicultural communities—that the city saw a significant surge in melded recipes. Eventually, these exotic flavors moved to cities north and south of Lisbon like Porto, integrating into the culinary fabric of each one.

The shining example is *frango no churrasco*, a Portuguese-African creation of chargrilled chicken smothered in piri-piri. Today, piri-piri hot sauce is a staple in any Portuguese condiment aisle, not to mention a gorgeous dried spice to keep on hand should the moment arise!

If you want to taste succulent Portuguese chicken, simply lift your nose skyward and let your stomach guide you to a smoky, hot *churrasco*. *Churrasco* is an umbrella term for grilled foods in both Spanish

Frango no churrasco (spicy chargrilled chicken) is an interesting example of Portugal's fusion cuisine.

and Portuguese, while a *churrasqueira* is where you can savor these mouthwatering bits of charred perfection. Though unlike Brazil, where waiters cut juicy slices of meat directly off a skewer and onto your plate, here you'll find a *churrasqueira* serves grilled chicken.

The *churrasqueira* is technically Portugal's original fast-food joint. Well before McDonald's et al., families turned to *frango no churrasco* as an easy dinner solution. In fact, the majority still do! For less than five euros, you can savor an entire butterflied chicken, marinated in garlic and herbs and grilled over a charcoal fire, alongside a salad, rice, and French fries. And when they ask if you want *molho* (spicy sauce)—the answer is, yes! This sauce is a tame, if not introverted, cousin to its Mexican or Indian brethren, so don't be shy and apply liberally.

Prefer a darker meat? Enter the duck or quail. The duck rice dish of *arroz de pato* is a staple of rustic Portuguese cuisine and common on restaurant menus. It requires layering shredded duck and rice in an earthenware dish to bake before finishing with an egg wash, slices of *chouriço* (smoked sausage),

The Portuguese adoration for chicken pales in comparison to their love of eggs. In times when meat was scarce, families turned to eggs as their source of protein, concocting comfy recipes like *ervilhas com ovos escalfados* (stewed peas, bacon, and poached eggs).

Made with bird's eye chilies, say YES to the spicy piri-piri on your chicken.

Stop at Bem-Me-Quer
in Braga for succulent,
old-fashioned duck rice.

and freshly chopped parsley. This is a signature dish of Braga (an hour north of Porto), where you can find *arroz de pato à antiga*, which combines the meat and rice instead of layering them and has a final coating of *cupita* (smoked meat made from *porco Bísaro*, see Meat on page 158).

Arroz de pato profoundly influenced one of the hottest dishes at Aldea in New York City, the Michelin-starred restaurant owned by Portuguese American Chef George Mendes. It's a whimsical interpretation of the original recipe with candied duck skin and molecular olives that playfully blends rustic and refined flavors.

Along with duck, the chef features quail in his cookbook, *My Portugal*. Enjoying this dainty bird requires time and a scalpel to surgically remove the succulent meat attached to its tiny bones. It's an ode to patience! A cross between a Cornish hen and partridge, these birds are usually served as *petiscos* among a table of family and friends. Think of the convivial spirit of breaking open steamed crabs. The quail are generally pickled overnight in *vinha d'alhos*, then fried in batches and piled into a pan with the reserved marinade to simmer. The result is addictive. When you go to Conga in Porto, ask for their braised quail as a side to a decadent *bifana* (pork sandwich), the house specialty. Though cartoonish, with its wee legs pointing upward on a bare plate, the tender quail meat is heavenly.

Nearly 10 years younger than Lucinda, Marília Brandão is just as passionate about the market as her elder counterpart. When it comes to Marília, it's all zen and goddess energy. She's lighthearted, flowing, and has a smile capable of ending world strife. We're 99% convinced that she's hiding a glittery pair of wings under her starched white apron. Try clicking your heels together in front of her to see what happens—you never know!

And like all good fairies, Marília is busy making the world a better place. She's off whispering sweet nothings to market cats or cooing over children. Often, you'll find her propped serenely on the grand staircase, hands poised neatly behind her back, telepathically communicating with each and every plant about the joys of life. She makes the Good Witch of the North seem paltry.

If you see frango *on one menu and* galinha *on another for the same dish—don't panic! Yes, they're both chicken;* frango *is a younger bird.*

Slender with high cheekbones and a bouncy, cottony white bob, Marília is so delicate and pretty that you would want to put her on a pedestal instead of a poultry stand. One of her family's longtime friends, a local doctor, was equally challenged by the notion of her being at the market and insisted that Marília (then in her late teens) work at his laboratory instead. She did, but on Saturdays when the lab closed at 1 p.m., Marília would dash to the market where she felt at home. She spent nearly seven years at the lab before opting to stay full time in Bolhão, where she worked inside the slaughterhouse adjacent to her stand (it's now a storage room). "I always wanted to be here, because I truly like it," says Marília. "To me, this place was so marvelous."

At one point, Bolhão and the market at Bom Sucesso were the only places with slaughterhouses in the city of Porto. Bolhão even had its own veterinarian that examined and stamped each animal for quality assurance, motivating businesses of all stripes—restaurants, banquet halls, and hotels—to rely on the market for orders. Eventually, the *matadouro* (slaughterhouse) left the market and opened up businesses elsewhere in the city, selling directly to the customers that once frequented Bolhão. This was an enormous blow to business owners like Marília who depended on Bolhão's slaughterhouse to meet customer demand. In its heyday, Bolhão had about 15 vendors selling poultry, much of it live. But today, only Marília and Lucinda are at the market regularly. Marília has opted to get her poultry (and some rabbits) already slaughtered from purveyors she trusts. It was a practical move, but she sincerely misses the connection she once felt to her poultry.

The vibrancy and passion of women like Lucinda and Marília is what attracts people from all walks of life to the market. Bolhão is an ecosystem of contrasts, where love and loss, life and death, animals and people converge. It's the cycle of life concentrated in one exceptional place.

"We get a lot of university students in here. One time during pledge week, a large group of students marched in and lined up on this grand staircase," recounts Marília, pointing to the steps as if reliving the moment. "Each one carried a toothbrush. They had been instructed to sweep clean the staircase with the tiny brushes. Oh Lord, the things I have witnessed in here. It's such a riot!"

It has always been this way, we're told. Staring up at the sky, Lucinda's eyes burn with fire and sensuality as she recalls the numerous air force captains that would frequent the market specifically to see their pouty-lipped poultry queen. "Back then, we were beauties," she reminisces. "Me and another girl were two of the favorites. We were so popular that they featured us in commercials to promote the market at theaters." Replace her pilled wool sweaters for a vintage tea dress with open-toe shoes and we trust our hatchet-wielding dame would have given Ava Gardner a run for her money.

The enormous pride the vendors have for life spent inside the market overflows when they share their stories. That's why it's so significant to capture their tales—a piece of history. So, despite all the talk of slaughter and death, there's nothing morbid about Lucinda and Marília. Quite the opposite—it's life at its fullest.

When choosing a fresh chicken, look for skin that is neither transparent nor patchy—and run if there's a rancid odor!

Beyond her magnetic beauty, Marília Brandão is pure grace.

HERBS

Imagine a huge canvas of multidimensional textures, a vibrant masterpiece that never stops changing, moving, or recreating itself. The North of Portugal is the antithesis of sterile—it's an unending collage bursting with life. Fresh lavender spills over stone walls, rosemary peeks through cracked cement, and savory thyme snakes its way into abandoned lots. Where man strives to control the elements, Mother Nature impregnates the landscape with sweet aromas of eucalyptus, licorice, and magnolia.

In the North, famous for its schizophrenic microclimates, you'll find a wide range of herbs habitually used to cure everything from the common cold to gout and laryngitis, but only two are mainstays in the cuisine. Aside from the occasional cameo from *coentros* (cilantro) and *hortelã* (mint), it's sprigs of *salsa* (parsley) and the *folha de louro* (bay leaf) that are generously used to flavor soups, invigorate roasts, and revive marinades. Consider them the brick-and-mortar herbs to every Northern Portuguese dish.

If you're a lover of thyme, look for *tomilho bela luz*, or Spanish thyme. Beyond its strong camphor aroma, this hearty perennial is revered for its healing properties as a digestive, an antiseptic, and a substitute for salt—critical for those among us that cherish an extra sprinkle of salt in their food but can't have it. For the landlocked people of Trás-os-Montes (with limited access to the salt-producing villages on the coast) this local herb became a sustainable solution to flavor their foods. Another popular herb is the *segurelha,* a savory herb used in soups and bean dishes that comforts the soul while countering flatulence. It also happens to be an aphrodisiac, nicknamed the "Viagra of the poor" for anyone interested in an organic remedy to rekindle their love life. Now that's a super herb!

When you're in Porto, take a taxi ride to the lush herbal oasis of Cantinho das Aromáticas nestled deep inside Vila Nova de Gaia. With hundreds of culinary and medicinal herbs blanketing the land, it's not only eye candy, but a full-on university course on herbal plants.

Salsa (parsley) is the hardest-working herb in Northern cuisine.

RECIPES AND RECOMMENDATIONS

Bem-Me-Quer
CAMPO DAS HORTAS 5, BRAGA
+351 253 262 095

Want to feel royal and rustic all at once? Hop on the train from Porto heading north to the Baroque city of Braga and hit up the vibrant dining scene bubbling amid the most palatial streets of Portugal. There, you'll find the restaurant Bem-Me-Quer, where rustic dishes are served in a light and airy space. Dig into premium cured meats made from the Bísaro pig before enjoying iconic Minho dishes, such as *bacalhau à Braga* (cured cod fried and topped with caramelized onions) and *arroz de pica no chão*. The latter, named after the free-range hens of Minho, is a regional interpretation of *arroz de cabidela* (rice enriched with chicken's blood). At the top of our list is the *arroz de pato à antiga,* a luscious version of Portuguese duck rice. Curious about the so-called bacon pudding, the *pudim Abade de Priscos* (see Pastries & Coffee on page 194)? Well then, this is an excellent spot to taste it.

ARROZ DE PATO À ANTIGA
(Old-Fashioned Duck Rice)

Yield: 3 servings
Time: 1 hour

1 whole duck, trimmed of excess fat
½ cured pig's ear or strip of cured pork belly
½ pound cured ham
1 *chouriço* (smoked sausage), sliced into rounds, divided
Freshly ground black pepper, to taste
1 clove
Coarse salt, to taste
Extra virgin olive oil
1 large yellow onion, chopped
4 cloves garlic, minced
2 cups uncooked *agulha* (long-grain) rice
1 tablespoon unsalted butter
1 bunch flat-leaf parsley

1. Preheat the oven to 375°F.

2. In a large pot set over medium heat, combine the duck, pig's ear, cured ham, *chouriço* (reserve a few slices to top the dish), black pepper, and clove. Add salt as needed, since the cured meats add salt already. Add enough water to cover and bring to a boil and cook until the cured meats start to break apart and the duck is tender. Set aside and reserve the broth.

3. In another pan, add enough olive oil to coat and set it over medium heat until the oil begins to bubble. Add the chopped onion and minced garlic and cook, stirring frequently, until golden. Add the broth and simmer until it thickens a bit.

4. Remove the duck meat from the bones and discard the bones. Shred the meat and combine it in a bowl with the cured meat drippings.

5. Cook the rice according to package directions. Transfer the cooked rice into a *caçarola do Minho* (deep ceramic dish), add the butter, and fold in the onion-broth mixture and the meat mixture. Bake for about 20 minutes.

6. Remove from the oven. Garnish with parsley and the reserved slices of *chouriço.* Serve.

Cantinho do Avillez

RUA DE MOUZINHO DA SILVEIRA, 166 R/C, PORTO
+351 223 227 879

The young world-renowned chef behind Belcanto in Lisbon, a restaurant with two Michelin stars, opened his namesake Cantinho do Avillez in Porto as a passion project. Located downhill from the historic São Bento train station on Mouzinho da Silveira, Cantinho do Avillez is cozy and unassuming and fits perfectly into the cascading tiled walls of Porto's Baixa (Downtown). With mismatched vintage chairs surrounding chunky white tables and crimson banquettes with rustic cutting boards and antique utensils hanging above them, you can't help but settle in and feel perfectly at home. Yet unlike the familiar feel, the menu seamlessly fuses traditional Portuguese cuisine with exotic flavors from Chef José Avillez's worldly travels to the Middle and Far East, including dishes such as crispy game sausage with soft-boiled egg; smoked tomato and rapini rice; sautéed scallops with trout eggs; and asparagus, saffron, and lemon risotto. If you have to choose one not-to-miss dish, go for the sautéed poultry liver with onion and Port marmalade. Served in a copper pan, this sweet and savory dish will entice even those normally averse to offal.

FIGADOS DE AVES SALTEADOS EM UVAS E PORTO

(Sautéed Poultry Livers with Grapes and Port)

Yield: 4 servings
Time: 50 minutes

14 ounces chicken livers
6 tablespoons white Port
3 cloves garlic, slightly crushed
3 sprigs fresh thyme
Whole black peppercorns, to taste
½ cup olive oil
¾ cup ruby Port
12 red grapes, halved and deseeded
Sea salt and freshly ground black
 pepper, to taste

1. Clean the livers of nerves and fat. Transfer them to a bowl, add the white Port, garlic, thyme, and whole peppercorns, and marinate for 30 minutes.

2. Place the oil in a nonstick frying pan, add the marinated livers, and sauté them over high heat until golden brown and caramelized on both sides. Lower the heat to medium, drizzle the livers with the ruby Port, and let the sauce reduce for about 3 minutes, or until slightly thickened.

3. Remove the pan from the heat. Add the grapes and stir everything together. Season with salt and freshly ground black pepper. Transfer the livers, grapes, and sauce to a platter and serve immediately.

CHAPTER 5

MEAT

*"**Vitela Maronesa** is by far my favorite Portuguese meat due to its profound milky flavor and huge cooking diversity."*

—CHEF KIKO MARTINS

IF YOU MISS the butcher shops inside the market, you might think that men—other than the guys at the charcuterie Salsicharia Leandro, sandwiched between fish and produce stands—are forbidden to enter the female den of vendors. They aren't! It's merely a question of finding where the testosterone thrives, which is fittingly among the hanging meat.

On the mezzanine, along the intricate wrought iron banisters and checkered cement flooring, you'll stumble upon our protagonists. Consider them your mad scientists of meat. They're men with a mission, practiced in the art of hauling entire ox carcasses down packed corridors while blood generously drips down their worn, white lab coats. In any other context, they would make "killer" characters for a Stephen King film—but fortunately for us, they're our meat mavens.

Their isolated domain, a quiet sanctuary of meat, overlooks the entire market. While fishwives sing their seductive *pregão* and restaurants chant their menu of the day, only the whack of steel on bone can be heard above, on the second floor. Aside from a handful of produce vendors, the retro *manteigaria* (butter shop) kiosk run by a widow that sells an incredible *chouriço de vinho*, and a restaurant specializing in roasted suckling pig, only three butchers remain.

In an age when meat is shipped in from unknown locations, under equally unknown conditions, it's close to impossible to know what you're consuming. But in Bolhão, everything is on display! From cow tongue and pork loin to rabbit and goat, you can almost pinpoint where it took its last breath and with whom. This is art, not an obligation. These aren't bored factory workers with a ciggy hanging loosely from the corner of their lips; they're passionate sculptors who love to cook.

During Carnival season, it's tradition to eat insane amounts of *feijoada* and *cozido* (meat stews) to fill your reserves prior to fasting for Lent.

Alexandre Araújo—a total silver fox—has one of the most impressive butcher block collections we've ever seen. These thick, gorgeous chunks of wood have been loved for so long that they've taken on a personality of their own. They're smooth, sensual, and captivating. You're compelled to run your fingers over the undulating grooves that mark Alexandre's quick cuts and pressured balance.

The butcher blocks you'll find in the market are generally single stumps of wood, not composites, made of willow and eucalyptus. Considered hardwoods, they tend to be tight grained to prevent food particles from getting trapped and bacteria from having a field day on your beautiful cuts.

While wielding, and perpetually sharpening, a sleek ICEL butcher knife—the preferred Portuguese brand among market butchers—Alexandre enthusiastically shares his joy for making Porto's signature stew *tripas à moda do Porto*, or simply, *tripas*. As legend has it, the dish received its name during the Age of Discovery, when the Portuguese royal military ordered the people of Porto to give up their carnivorous habits for their brethren fighting in Africa. The people obliged and were solely left with the entrails, or offal. Since then, the people of Porto have been called Tripeiros (Tripe Eaters), a moniker they embrace as a symbol of their strong regional identity.

The undulating grooves on Alexandre Araújo's timeworn cutting board are captivating.

Top to bottom right:

Alexandre Araújo takes a phone order from a loyal customer; Alexandre Araújo cubes meat for *jardineira* (beef stew); *tripas à moda do Porto*, the city's signature tripe stew.

Top to bottom right:

The *favos de mel* (honeycomb) tripe is the top choice for the stew recipe of *tripas à moda do Porto*; Alexandre Araújo keeps his washed tripe in a lemon bath; *cozido à moda do Minho,* rustic meat stew.

With beehive nooks and crannies, favos de mel
(honeycomb tripe) is a patchwork of flavor-absorbing
sponge cups.

For the less squeamish among you, this velvety stew is phenomenal for cold winter nights. It's homey, rich comfort food made with cow (or veal) intestine, hooves, pig's ear, cured meats, chicken, white beans, carrots, onions, cumin, pepper, and parsley. Three types of tripe are generally used—*favos de mel* (honeycomb), *folhos* (folds), and *pança* (belly). The honeycomb tends to be at the top of the list for its thinness, but whatever the choice, the tripe must be washed several times before being scrubbed in a salt, vinegar, and lemon bath. Scalded and rewashed, it's then soaked in cold water overnight before cooking. In Alexandre's shop, a white plastic bin filled with tripe soaking with rounds of lemon will "cheerfully" greet you at the door. Welcome to Porto!

You can also savor the North's most cherished stew, the *cozido à moda do Minho.* This snout-to-tail lover's dream has everything you can possibly imagine. A mix of meats, vegetables, smoked sausages, and practically every part of the pig is successively thrown into a pot of boiling water to create one of the most unattractive yet flavorful dishes you'll ever taste. Leftovers can be transformed into *feijoada à Transmontana,* similar to *tripas à moda do Porto* sans the tripe and with a wider blend of meats. In Bolhão, the Portuguese can find each and every one of these ingredients, customarily prepared by affectionate matriarchs for their large family gatherings.

This gift for transforming frugal foods into wholesome dishes is deeply seeded in the Portuguese psyche, but it reaches its pinnacle with meat. At the request of a portly woman whose brows barely make it over the counter, Alexandre reaches for a wobbly liver inside the glass case and drops it on his warped cutting board. "Make sure they're thin," she dictates, pushing herself up on her tiptoes, "very thin!" Her unabashed plea is the coveted secret behind *iscas com elas,* a homestyle meal of fried liver steaks soaked overnight in *vinha d'alhos* (see Poultry on page 119), topped with slightly caramelized onions, and served with boiled potatoes.

These thrifty *tasca* (tavern) recipes are a product of living nearly half a century under a dictator regime, followed by years of catching up to the rest of Europe, and most recently, juggling a Eurozone crisis. Portuguese families never had much room to flex their financial muscles when buying beef. Outside of cattle-rearing regions, where thick steaks were more affordable, Portuguese ingenuity cooked up *bifes de cebolada*—paper-thin beef cutlets braised in wine and onions until tender—and *jardineira* (beef stew). You'll also see *língua de vaca estufada* (stewed cow tongue) or *rabo de boi* (oxtail) on the menu of many homestyle restaurants, ensuring that nothing goes to waste. One thing's for sure, there's never been a shortage of creative ways to cook up meats in Portugal. You can even order a *bife na pedra*, raw beef on a sizzling stone with bowls of sauces, and sear it yourself.

These days, you'll find retouched versions of traditional recipes at revitalized *tascas* (a major trend), where Portuguese foodies are seeking out their grandmother's cuisine in refreshed settings. The common thread to these dishes is patience. Instead of 10-minute meals, meats are marinated in *vinha d'alhos* for 24 hours and slow cooked, resulting in rich, aromatic sauces.

Savory pastries are another way the Portuguese incorporate beef into their eating habits. One of the most revered in the North is the *pastel de Chaves*, a 150-year-old recipe for puff pastry stuffed with ground veal from the Trás-os-Montes city of Chaves. Legend has it that in 1862, an anonymous woman started selling these flaky crescent pastries from a basket on the streets of Chaves—and people couldn't get enough of them! She sold her recipe to one of the local bakeries, Casa do Antigo Pasteleiro, where it grew in popularity and eventually surfaced in mainstream markets. To protect its methods of preparation and origins, the *pastel de Chaves* has been certified with a seal of authenticity. You'll likely find these savory treats at some of the bread vendors inside Bolhão or most of the pastry shops that dot

Left to right:

Cubed beef for stews; chargrilled *entrecosto* (ribs).

Chargrilled *posta de vitela Mirandesa,* one of the DOP meats of the North.

Porto. The most coveted shop is the Loja dos Pastéis de Chaves, which has several locations; however, the one on Rua da Firmeza is a delightful choice. The Loja also whips up vegetarian and sweet pastries.

Though gigantic marbled cuts of beef aren't the norm on most Portuguese tables, exceptions are made in ranching regions where premium products are produced and consumed regularly. North of Porto, you'll find Maronesa (the Kobe beef of Portugal) from the cattle grazing the Marão mountains as well as Mirandesa and Barrosã in Minho and Trás-os-Montes, all sealed DOP (protected designation of origin). The latter is the meat that popularized Portuguese beef on London menus as a result of the exports of this high-quality product from Portugal to English courts during the 19th century. In and around the town of Arouca (an hour south of Porto), restaurants specialize in a variation of beef dishes with another prized DOP meat called Arouquesa. These include chargrilled steaks or chops that require only the right amount of coarse salt and red-hot embers to deliver succulent meat to the table, ranging from *vaca* (cow), *boi* (ox), and *novilho* (calf, nine to 24 months) to *vitela* (veal, six to nine months) and *vitelão* (veal, six to 13 months). A quiet shift for these meats, from niche to mainstream, is gradually becoming palpable. The game changers are the Portuguese chefs, especially Michelin starred and celebrity, who have garnered interest for DOP meats on their menus and organized tasting events to educate the public about them. This rise in curiosity has resulted in new meat-focused restaurants, including top steak houses, opening their doors in both Lisbon and Porto. Even the most traditional butcher shops in Porto, like Alexandre's, show signs that a beef renaissance is surging in Portugal. Customers are asking him to age their meat in the shop for days on end, while

Mirandesa bovines, recognized by the curly locks between their horns, were once used to pull fishing boats from the water.

local winemakers are on the hunt for marbled meat to barbeque in the Douro. After years of national health cries for leaner meats (a.k.a government scare tactics), butchers are welcoming eager requests for quality upgrades. Bring on the steak!

As we banter away with Alexandre, a young woman with spiky, punk blonde hair saunters through the door, not in search of steak, but of a stand instead. "We get young people in here all the time looking for space to open up a business. They're educated youngsters with good ideas," he says. Yet, City Hall won't allow newcomers to open up shop, a major reason, he explains, for the demise of Bolhão. "It's important to attract young residents to the city; it should have been done 30 years ago. Oftentimes, it's not that the rents are that expensive, the issue is that many of these apartments need to be restored. There are shopping centers that opened up because it was trendy, but they could have been used for housing instead. City Hall should have realized this wasn't the right approach. We had enough commerce here, what we needed were more residents." We couldn't agree more with Alexandre, and we're hopeful that Bolhão receives the restoration it deserves, a project that empowers the vendors and the entire city instead of threatening the traditions and stories that have been safeguarded in this market for years.

Alexandre shakes his head disappointedly and mutters "*político*" under his breath. We let him vent. Understandably, he's distrustful. But as mindsets seem to be shifting, this might just be the right time for positive change to impact Bolhão. There's an entirely new generation of people who are hungry for sustainable food systems, which not only feed the body but the soul as well.

As for the butchers, they're overflowing with meaty stories and clever conversations. Here, you'll meet Portugal's war veterans, amateur soccer players, and café politicians. These are the men that congregate at their neighborhood social club to read newspapers and discuss current events while playing canasta or dominoes. They're the Portuguese uncles that sit you on their knee and widen your imagination with their fervent views of the world. Conversations with these discerning men will transport you to the colonial wars and the Carnation Revolution. (Portugal overthrew the Salazar regime, the dictatorship that ran the country for nearly 50 years, through a military coup in 1974.) Though they're passionate about the market, the country, and current affairs in general, the butchers are also extremely humble and gentle, not a surprise for a generation of men that preferred the thin green stem of a red carnation in their guns over bullets. They tear up easily at the mention of their beloved yet decaying Bolhão, resenting past city governments for the mismanagement of the situation.

With a heavy heart, Alcino Fernando Moreira Sousa quickly turns to pick up a four-inch binder sitting alone on a marble counter next to a picture of Our Lady of Fátima and a bright yellow sign with the words "I asked God for advice to find joy. God showed me the land and said work, sow, and create." It's clear to us that the pages inside this binder are the seeds Alcino has been attempting to sow in order to reap a better future for the market. With long strides to match his towering size, he gently carries it over as if it were his Bible, neatly stacked with piles of letters that he has sent to Porto's City Hall and to Lisbon (the nation's capital) in search of answers for the market.

Alcino was once the president of a strong vendor association inside the market. With each and every promise the government broke over the course of 30 years, divisions and distrust among the vendors widened, weakening the association to the point of practically dissolving it.

"In the good sense of the word, I'm a revolutionary. I always like to see things done with equality. When I don't see this, I get frustrated," says Alcino, flipping through the pages of the binder to show us the most significant letters. "I still haven't abandoned the association because I don't want to be accused of not doing enough."

Despite the ongoing disputes and disillusionment within the market, the vendors remain determined to fight for it. Understandably so, considering the emotional and financial investment involved. For nearly three decades, Alcino has run the most spacious butcher shop inside Bolhão. Among other meats, he promotes *cabrito* (three-month-old kid or suckling goat) from the steep, waterfall-laden cliffs of Armamar. Located two hours southeast of Porto in the district of Viseu, where Northern and Central cuisines merge, this area has the landscape that goats dream of. Alexandre equally touts the goat from the municipality of Mogadouro, northeast of Porto and part of Bragança deep into Trás-os-Montes.

Though a Lisbon specialty, the dish of iscas *(liver cutlets)* com elas *(with them) is an all-around favorite these days in Porto. The* elas *are the potatoes!*

Former president of one of the vendor associations inside Bolhão, Alcino Fernando Moreira Sousa has spent years sending letters to City Hall about the poor state of the market.

When buying kid (not as in child trafficking, but as in suckling goat), make sure the spine is white and the bones are bright red. It's also a good sign if the animal's offal is glossy and intact.

Regardless of geography, goat is a favorite among the Portuguese, instigating dozens of creative dishes based on our four-legged friend. In Minho, there's a decadent (or perhaps, "indecent") roasting recipe with a name that might get you in trouble. It's called *foda à moda de Monção*, loosely translated as "fucked over Monção style." As local legend has it, fair merchants would lace their goat feed with salt, causing an unquenchable thirst among the innocent livestock. The more they drank, the larger their bellies became, impressing gullible farmers on the hunt for hefty animals. Once they realized that they had been fooled, they would exclaim, "*Foda à Monção!*" Over the years, the saying was adapted to the recipe, referring to goat roasted in the town of Monção. In other places, you might see the G-rated version of this recipe name as *cabrito à moda de Monção* (goat Monção style). But that's way too tame for Minhotos, the fierce folks of Minho!

Though *cordeiro* (lamb) might also be used, the recipe traditionally calls for goat. The meat is liberally rubbed with an herbed garlic paste and left to sit overnight. The following day, a second rub of

Alcino Fernando Moreira Sousa advertises on his store window goat from Armamar, touted as one of the best.

Opposite, top to bottom:

Paprika, lemon juice, and coarse salt are fundamental ingredients in meat recipes.

saffron is applied before piercing the meat with pockets of cured ham and pork belly. Now, sigh and drool insatiably while you wait for the meat to finish roasting—which may feel like a lifetime.

Alcino preps his goat by soaking it in a lemon bath for a half hour to tame the gamey flavor and remove any impurities. He then dumps the water and marinates the goat overnight in garlic, spices, and Vinho Verde or beer. The following day, it's slowly roasted.

Clearly exhausted and worn out, every ounce of Alcino's being has been poured into this market. His heart throbs from every tile, his tears stream from every rivet. But with just one whisper of hope, he comes alive. His willful nature leaves little room for sulking; instead, he would rather focus on the future. Pointing to a mock drawing of the market on his wall, he explains how a private group was interested in buying Bolhão, but the deal sparked heated contention among the vendors who vehemently protested the installation of a supermarket chain.

But not everyone shared this fear. Sitting alone in the cavernous back corner of the mezzanine, where a flat-screen television plays the daily news, we find António José Ferreira Moreira lounging in a plastic chair. António is soft on the inside, the type of guy you could enjoy a beer with, but he's not without opinions. He couldn't care less about the supermarket chain, claiming anything's better than the current dilapidation of the market. "What's the problem with having a supermarket chain in here?" he questions in defiance. "There are already so many others at our doorstep. The difference would be that people would actually come inside the market and see

that there are traditional butcher shops that know how to compete with these supermarket chains. Customers would realize that with us they have better choices. What's the point of having fine veal here if nobody comes inside to see it?"

António's defeated demeanor immediately changes when we ask if he enjoys cooking. His slouched shoulders suddenly stretch and straighten as he tells us about the *pitéus* (lip-smacking bites) he whips up for lunch in the back of his shop. *Rojões* are one of his favorites, marbled pork cubes cut from the pig's leg. But instead of preparing the traditional and labor-intensive *rojões à moda do Minho,* he seasons the pork cubes with garlic and wine and lets them sit for a few minutes in an old mug before searing the meat in a worn skillet with olive oil. Diced onions are tossed in to caramelize, and the final concoction is thrown over plain rice. "It's *rojões* my way!" he blares out, which makes us smile, thinking of all the Portuguese men we've met that are blessed with this talent of cutting corners on intricate recipes to create pure savory candy in the kitchen. Their secret seems to lie in halting the cooking process soon after the tastiest part: the sear! Whether it's genius or laziness, the result is utter indulgence.

Left to right:

António José Ferreira Moreira splits a hoof; chops it; and torches it.

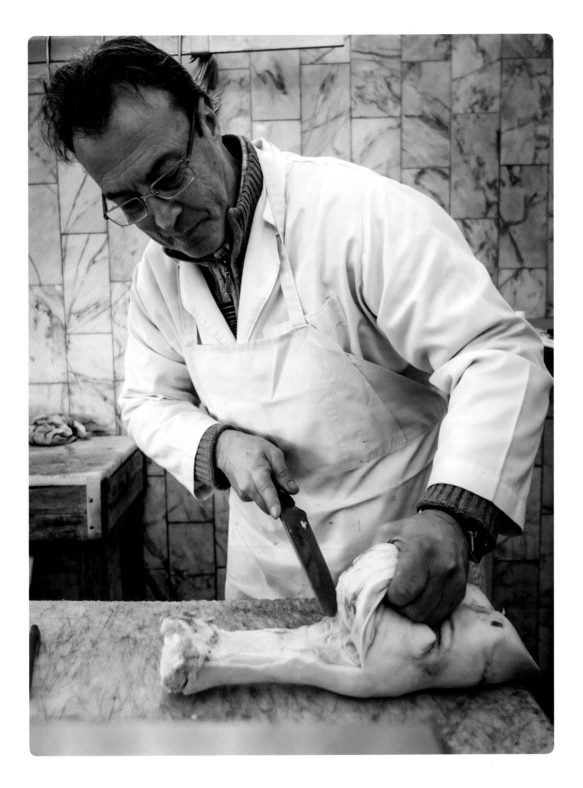

In a bygone Portugal, what wasn't consumed in the meat industry was turned into a byproduct (e.g., ox hooves for buttons).

António José Ferreira Moreira preps a hoof to use in rustic stews.

Cut into bite-size pieces, the *redenho* (belly fat) is transformed into pork cracklings and thrown into Minho's extreme meat dish of *rojões*.

The traditional dish, however, takes tons more effort and is entirely more extreme—a characteristic of many of the meat dishes of the North. The dish varies depending on which city, town, or village you pick to devour it in—Ponte de Lima in Minho is a foodie top choice. The pork cubes are marinated overnight, and the next day seared in lard and then simmered until tender. It's served with a series of pork derivatives, including fried *tripa enfarinhada* (tripe stuffed with seasoned flour) and slices of *belouras*, a loaf of blended rye, wheat, cornmeal, and pig's blood—it's something scrapple lovers might enjoy. This messy yet delicious medley of pork bits is served with one, or all, of the following side dishes: roasted potatoes, chestnuts, *arroz de sarrabulho*—a mixture of rice, shredded fresh and smoked meats, pig's blood, cornmeal, onions, spices, and wine. Did we mention this meal is not for the fainthearted?

Unique to the North, *tripa enfarinhada* is pork intestine stuffed with cornmeal flour, cumin, and black pepper. It's fried until slightly crispy.

The word prego (nail) in prego no pão (steak sandwich) refers to the flank cut, which hardens as nails if overcooked.

Topped with a fried egg, *prego no pão* is Portugal's steak sandwich.

Though Portugal certainly boasts a diverse repertoire of meat dishes, absolutely nothing beats its masterfulness with pork. Chefs suggest that pork lends itself well to the all-around Portuguese resourcefulness and inventiveness, which is especially evident in the kitchen. American celebrity chef Emeril Lagasse (half Portuguese) dubbed this as "Portuguese ingenuity." The number of recipes the Portuguese have created from pork is indeed impressive. Whether it's elaborate regional stews, sinful sandwiches, smoked sausages, or a crackling fire pit with roasted suckling pig (we're seriously only scratching the surface), a pork pilgrimage to Portugal should be on every gastrotourist bucket list.

At the butcher shops, you'll see tiny, handwritten signs promoting ultra-thin pork cutlets destined for Portugal's most popular fast food, *bifanas*. These succulent sandwiches are made by simmering the pork in garlic wine juices, hot sauce, and for the more traditional, lard! Dripping in sauce, this über-tender meat is shoved inside a Portuguese roll and washed down with an ice-cold beer. Still, the "signature sandwich" for Porto is unequivocally the *francesinha*, but we'll let you drool over that one in the chapter on cured meat (page 178).

The most nascent craze is the *sandes de pernil*, a combination of fresh and cured pig's shank that's slow roasted, pulled, and typically served with a generous slice of Serra da Estrela cheese, which is native to the Center region of Portugal, but often found in Porto. Also hailing from the Center is *leitão à moda da Bairrada*, a roasted two- to six-month-old milk-fed piglet that'll make your soul weep and your taste buds sing. Nelson Lopes brings whole roasted suckling pigs to Bolhão on Tuesday, Wednesday, Friday, and Saturday from his hometown in Bairrada, where he runs a few other restaurants on top of Nelson dos Leitões inside the market. Porto has a strong affinity for suckling pig from the heartland of Portugal; hence, it was a no-brainer to open up a restaurant in Bolhão. Since then, Nelson's gained fame for his perfectly spiced and succulent *leitão*—not to mention his bibelot collection of shagging pigs! Take time to enjoy his juicy and perfectly spiced *leitão* sandwich on-site—a sumptuous treat that's considerably better than his take-home frozen alternative.

Nelson recalls the insane bustle inside the market when he opened his doors in 1991. "It took us more than 15 minutes just to get the pigs from the delivery van and through the crowds to get inside the market," he says. Though the multitudes in the market have died down, Nelson has maintained a loyal clientele at his place. "Today, thank God, we have a good reputation."

Top to bottom:

Roasted suckling pig
sandwich from Nelson
dos Leitões; *pernil* (cured
pig's knee) sandwich
from Lareira with melting
wedge of mountain cheese.

Though a series of *leitão* houses have sprouted over the years, many of them, according to Nelson, use electric ovens. His pigs are roasted the old-fashioned way in a wood-powered stone oven in Bairrada. Other than the appropriate oven and seasoning (loads of garlic, pepper, and lard), it's also important to use the best breed for this dish, the Bísaro pig raised in the North and parts of the Center. No sweat for Nelson—his brother-in-law has his own Bísaro farm! At Bolhão, Nelson has help from his son Nuno Lopes, and together they delight patrons who appreciate an authentic product without having to travel two hours to get it. "It's more expensive to use Bísaro, but it's tastier," explains Nelson. "I maintain the highest quality. Those that want to pay, pay, and those that don't can go get something cheaper." Between the puffs of smoke from his perpetual cigarette, Nelson never minces his words. Essentially, choosing the Bísaro breed is like choosing a cage-free hen over a domestic chicken. The pigs are raised on a natural diet of tubers, vegetables, fruits, and some grain while roaming spacious grounds. You can tell if the pig is low quality by the way the meat turns into a ball in your mouth, Nelson warns. Traditionally, *leitão* pairs with *espumante* from the Bairrada and a side of thick rounds of oranges. Both aid digestion, says Nelson, and the latter also serves as a palate cleanser.

Ready to be served! Pieces of *leitão assado no forno* (roasted suckling pig).

Nelson Lopes delights
Porto patrons with
authentic *Bairrada
leitão* (suckling pig).

Loyal customers are especially important to Nelson and António whose businesses are tucked into the sides of the market without entrances. To make matters worse, their entire wing of the building is empty of shops, causing a worrisome decline in traffic. But thankfully in Porto, a mouthwatering piece of roasted pig and an engaging butcher still mean something.

Spellbound by his agility and restlessness, we savor António's energetic spirit as he shares stories about his family and their connection to Bolhão. António's butcher shop belonged to his father, who played on the once vibrant soccer team Salgueiros. António is so smitten with his soccer heritage that he points to the chirping canary caged next to the door and boasts with a wry smile, "That's Messi." António's father started working in Bolhão when he was merely nine years old, and his mother ran a

Look up when strolling through Bolhão, because it's not only the vendors and their wares that are enticing, it's the retro signs as well.

produce stand inside the market that belonged to her grandmother. Eventually, the two fell in love, married, and started a family of their own. When he turned 17, António joined his father and the rest is history.

Back then, there weren't only *talhos* (butcher shops) and *salsicharias* (charcuteries), there were also places dedicated exclusively to *miudezas* (offal). These shops were run by women called *fressureiras* (the word derives from *fressura*, meaning "entrails"). In those days, if you needed cow intestine or tongue for your stew, these women were the suppliers, explains António. But when mad cow disease hysteria overtook Europe in the early 2000s, they were wiped out.

Male butchers handled gigantic cuts of meat, often too heavy for women, says Adelino José Almeida Santos, who ran a butcher shop with his wife, Inês Gomes Coelho, for nearly 30 years. This is one of the reasons why the butcher trade is dominated by men, he points out. "You might be handling a piece of meat that weighs one pound, and the next minute, you're working with meat that's 80 pounds or more," he says. "For women, this is a bit difficult." But when it comes to charming the customer, he says, there's nothing like a woman's touch.

"Women might linger around longer to chat if there's a woman behind the counter," Inês confirms from personal experience. A year after our interview with Adelino and Inês, the couple decided it was time to close up shop.

Though the rest of the butchers remain open and ready to welcome you, there's no shop as lively as Alexandre's, which is blessed with one of the friendliest employees in the market. Alexandre keeps his composure, answering our questions with the utmost serious tone, while in the backdrop the wide-smiling Carlos Leal softens the moment with a quirky story, then an idea. "Let's open up a restaurant together," Carlos winks at us from behind Alexandre, "a butcher shop that doubles as a restaurant. Makes sense, right?" Like sidekicks in a witty sitcom, the two unintentionally entertain their audience with a personal touch that goes well beyond the norm. This generosity might include providing pill-size pieces of raw liver for an anemic customer to swallow on demand. Ahh reality, you're so much sweeter than fiction.

The secret to pork secretos *lies in the cut: just near the belly where bacon also comes from. Enough said!*

As if the wide range of typical options weren't enough at these butcher shops, the diversity of meat in Portugal extends well beyond free range or farm raised. There's also a hunting heritage that brings to the table hearty wild meat recipes with everything from *coelho bravo* (wild rabbit) and *lebre* (hare) to *javali* (boar). Though you'll see some of these meats in Porto when they're in season, there's nothing like experiencing them in a rural setting. In Trás-os-Montes, the rabbit recipes can be as simple as layering pieces of the meat with sliced onions and parsley, drizzling it with local olive oil and white wine, and slow cooking for a few hours. Served with boiled potatoes, this dish is simple, rustic, and homey. More elaborate dishes might entail marinating the meat overnight, massaging in lard the next morning, and slow roasting in the oven in a cradle of pork belly. Vegetarians will live happily in these valleys and hilltops, too, since handpicking *cogumelos bravos* (wild mushrooms) for stews generally coincides with the hunting seasons.

And though not specifically a Northern dish, *coelho à caçador* (rabbit stew) is common on most menus countrywide as an ode to the *caçador* (hunter). Drenched in a rich tomato and wine sauce, this stew is heavenly with loads of crusty bread for dipping and sopping. During wild boar hunting season in Trás-os-Montes look for *javali no pote com castanhas*, wild boar stewed with chestnuts inside a cast-iron pot—a definite throwback to medieval Portugal.

Clearly, carnivores need not fear the land of cod and sardines. In fact, that would be misleading—Portugal has just as much to offer meat-adoring foodies as it does seafood lovers. That's why we cherish Bolhão's butchers; though they are significant to the country's identity, they remind us of a Portugal that's often overlooked. Despite tremendous coastal diversity and wealth, it has been the meat stew that for years sustained much of the country. Just as Bolhão's inconspicuous butchers are worth discovering, so is the meatier side of Portugal.

Carlos Leal, Alexandre Araújo's employee, keeps customers entertained with his jovial conversations.

RECIPES AND RECOMMENDATIONS

O Caraças
RUA DAS TAIPAS 27, PORTO
+351 220 174 505

Matriarchy and meat rule at O Caraças, loosely translating to "Screw it!" Tucked into an emblematic side street that steeply descends into the riverfront in downtown Porto, O Caraças is jam-packed with personality. You'll likely be greeted by Paula and Mónica Lage, two tiny, no-bullshit sisters who adore their mother's food as much as we do, as proven by their frequent trips into the kitchen for a quick nibble. That nibble is a direct result of Maria Luísa Lage's intrinsic ability to whip up succulent cuisine as she tends to her stove, precariously teetering on a step stool while simultaneously manning the heavy-duty smoker she uses to infuse woodsy traces into her juicy meats. With strong ties to Trás-os-Montes, where they get their mouthwatering Barrosã meats for dishes like the earthy *vitela Barrosã assada no forno*, this spacious spot fills up fast, so make a reservation. On warm nights, choose the relaxed outdoor terrace that offers an inspiring view of Porto.

VITELA BARROSÃ ASSADA NO FORNO
(Roasted Barrosã Veal)

Yield: 8 servings
Time: 1 hour 45 minutes

1¾ cups olive oil, any type, divided
3 medium yellow onions, sliced
4 cloves garlic, minced, divided
4 small *malaguetas*, seeded
1 bunch flat-leaf parsley, chopped
1 bunch thyme, chopped
1 sprig mint
1 bay leaf
6 pounds *pá de vitela* (veal shoulder blade), trimmed of excess fat
1 tablespoon Massa de Pimentão (recipe follows)
Salt, to taste
2 cups dry white wine or beer

1. Warm 1½ cups of the olive oil in a pot set over medium-high heat until it begins to bubble. Add the onions, 2 garlic cloves, *malaguetas*, parsley, thyme, mint, and bay leaf and cook, stirring frequently, until the onions caramelize. Rub the meat with the Massa de Pimentão, add the salt and wine, and reduce the heat to low. Cover and braise for about 1 hour. Remove the meat from the pot and reserve the caramelized onion mixture.

2. Preheat the oven to 365°F.

3. In an oven-safe dish, add the remaining ¼ cup of olive oil and the remaining 2 garlic cloves. Add the meat and rub it in the olive oil and garlic mixture. Pour in the caramelized onion mixture. Roast for 30 minutes.

4. Remove from the oven, slice, and serve.

MASSA DE PIMENTÃO
(Red Bell Pepper Paste)

Yield: About 1 cup
Time: 2 days

6 large red bell peppers, stems,
   seeds, and ribs removed and
   cut into 1-inch strips
3–4 tablespoons coarse salt
3 cloves garlic
½ cup olive oil, any type

1. Place a layer of the bell pepper strips into the bottom of a bowl and generously sprinkle with the salt. Repeat this process with the remaining bell pepper strips, salting in between each layer. Cover tightly with a towel and let cure in a cool area of the kitchen for at least 12 hours.

2. Preheat the oven to 325°F.

3. Drain the bell peppers of excess liquid and put them into an oven-safe dish or baking pan. Roast for 1 hour and 30 minutes.

4. Remove the peppers from the oven and set them aside to cool to room temperature. Peel off the skins. Transfer the peeled pepper strips to the bowl of a food processor. Add the garlic. Blend the mixture for 30 seconds, or until a thick paste forms. Add ¼ cup of the olive oil and blend again for another 30 seconds. Add the remaining ¼ cup of oil and blend for another minute, or until smooth.

5. To preserve, leave the garlic out and just add fresh garlic each time you use the paste. Store in a sterilized, airtight jar in the refrigerator for up to a month.

TIP: *Certain recipes suggest curing the peppers up to six days, but when you don't have enough time, 12 to 24 hours is sufficient. However, the longer you cure the more intense the flavor.*

A Cozinha do Manel
RUA DO HEROÍSMO 215, PORTO
+351 225 363 388

If you can't make it to the mountains for roasted kid or suckling goat, the next best things are the homestyle restaurants in Porto like A Cozinha do Manel. A bit off the beaten track near the Campanhã train station, it's worth making a reservation for a dinner of *cabrito assado no forno* with a group of friends who are game to finish off a small goat with roasted potatoes, spinach mousse, and saffron rice enhanced with goat offal and cured meats. Open for nearly 30 years, this family-operated restaurant roasts its goats in ceramic baking dishes that spend up to three hours in a wood-powered oven that slowly tenderizes the rich meat. The blue and white tiles on the walls and rustic mahogany touches add to the authentic Portuguese experience.

CABRITO ASSADO NO FORNO
(Roasted Suckling Goat)

Yield: 6 to 8 servings
Time: 2 hours 45 minutes

1 (8-pound) whole suckling goat, trimmed of excess fat and quartered
2 lemons, sliced into rounds
Salt, to taste
3 cloves garlic, minced
1 bunch flat-leaf parsley, chopped
2 bay leaves
2 leaves fresh mint
1 cup olive oil
1 cup lard
1 tablespoon paprika
2 large yellow onions, sliced
6 pounds baby white potatoes
1 cup dry white wine
½ cup lager beer
½ shot Scotch
Arroz de Forno dos Miúdos do Cabrito, for serving (recipe follows)

1. Place the goat in a large deep bowl or basin. Add the lemons and enough water to completely submerge the goat. Soak in the refrigerator for 10 to 12 hours to eliminate odors.

2. Make a *pasta para barrar carne* (meat rub) by combining the salt, garlic, parsley, bay leaves, mint, olive oil, lard, and paprika in a bowl. Mix until well combined.

3. Remove the goat from the lemon-water bath and dry it well. Massage it with the meat rub until thoroughly coated and allow to marinate in the refrigerator for 24 hours.

4. In lieu of the wood-burning oven used in the original recipe, preheat the oven to 320°F.

5. Place the onions evenly in the bottom of an oven-safe ceramic dish. Add the goat, potatoes, wine, and beer. Roast, uncovered, in the oven for 1 hour. Refresh the goat with the Scotch. Flip the goat over and roast for another hour, or until an instant-read thermometer registers 145°F when inserted into the thickest part of the meat.

6. Serve with Arroz de Forno dos Miúdos do Cabrito.

ARROZ DE FORNO DOS MIÚDOS DO CABRITO

(Oven-Baked Rice with Goat Offal)

Yield: 6 to 8 servings
Time: 1 hour 40 minutes

1 goat head, halved
Liver, heart, lungs, kidneys, and
    brain from 1 goat
8 cups water
Olive oil (enough to cover the
    bottom of a medium pot)
1 head garlic, minced
1 large yellow onion, sliced
6 bay leaves
1 bunch flat-leaf parsley, chopped
5 cups *agulha* (long-grain) rice
½ tablespoon saffron

1. Place the goat head, liver, heart, lungs, kidneys, and brain in a large pot set over medium-high heat. Add the water and bring to a boil. Cook for 30 minutes. Remove from the heat. Strain the broth and set it aside. Remove and discard the goat head. Dice the boiled liver, heart, lungs, kidneys, and brain.

2. Preheat the oven to 320°F.

3. Coat the bottom of a pot set over medium-high heat with olive oil and warm until it begins to bubble. Add the garlic, onion, bay leaves, and parsley and cook, stirring frequently, until the onion is golden. Add the diced liver, heart, lungs, and kidneys (set the brain aside), and stir to coat with the onion mixture. Transfer the offal mixture to a deep ceramic dish. Remove and discard the bay leaves. Add the rice (2 cups of broth for every cup of rice) and stir in the saffron. Blanket the rice with the diced brain.

4. Bake for 35 to 45 minutes, until the crust is golden and crispy.

CHAPTER 6

CURED MEAT

"If the symbol of working-class prosperity in this country [the United States] was once, as Herbert Hoover said, a chicken in every pot, then, unquestionably, in Portugal it's a dry-cured smoked sausage in every pan."

—DAVID LEITE, *THE NEW PORTUGUESE TABLE*

PORTUGAL'S ENDLESS REPERTOIRE of pork recipes is so incredibly diverse that you would rightfully assume that mastering pork has been the country's ultimate culinary mission. But as is the case with most Portuguese dishes, the pervasiveness of pork is a mere consequence of survival, born out of the age-old family tradition of farm raising a pig as a means of being self-sufficient.

Come late autumn, as the gentle hues of orange and red blanket the landscape, rural families begin recruiting friends and family for their annual *matança do porco*. If you're a city dweller, a pig slaughter might sound horrifically gory, but for rural families, it's a time of celebration. Amid the morning mist and the toll of a crowing rooster, the head of the household and a handful of his men assist the village's skilled *matador*, a revered role that's bestowed upon a chosen few. As little eyes peer from behind barn doors and chickens shriek in disquieted anticipation, women stand patiently in the shadows. This position isn't one of passivity, but of expertise. Dressed in ornately patterned aprons, they collect the pig's intestines and blood to create a range of Portuguese foods called *enchidos*, which include *presuntos* (cured hams) and an extensive line of sausages that are smoked over a bed of oak and chestnut branches in a *fumeiro* (smokehouse).

The Portuguese rub olive oil on their smoked sausages to prevent them from drying out. You can do the same at home and they'll last beautifully.

Though olive oil is the prime fat of choice, *banha* (lard) still has its place in several authentic Portuguese recipes.

Don't let the *cabeças de porco fumadas* (smoked pig heads) turn you away—instead, let them "welcome" you to a wide range of new flavors.

If you're feeling a bit queasy, you're not in the minority, because much of our food has been separated from its origin, cleaned and perfectly packaged so as to erase all traces of where it came from. But for rural families, this ritual has been celebrated since time immemorial, alongside a wholesome meal of stewed pork bites served with strong homemade wine and a side of folky jingles. What a contradiction, you might say, considering that death is at the centerpiece of this occasion, but for the Portuguese and their southern European kin, these animals are sacred precisely because they sustain life. Every element of the pig is venerated and transformed into a type of cured meat, infused into a rustic recipe, or featured in a trendy snout-to-tail menu that's acclaimed by farm-to-table chefs today. And we can assure you that this is no exaggeration—snout does show up in Portuguese stews!

Not that long ago, European law banned the *matança* as a result of government views on public health issues and animal rights. Today, the law is more flexible, allowing Portuguese families to raise and slaughter their pigs (and other animals) if exclusively for domestic consumption. Among a list of clauses, the law states that licensed organizations can also execute a traditional *matança* for cultural demonstrations. When we think of the infinite number of *fumeiro* festivals that take place each year throughout Portugal, it makes sense that the law would eventually bend to accommodate a tradition that's so integral to the fabric of Portuguese food. In the North, one of the most beloved festivals is held in the Trás-os-Montes village of Vinhais with the prized *porco Bísaro* at the heart of its smoky creations (see Meat on page 158).

At age 10, Maria Luísa Silva was handed a cleaver and a bone to kick off her lifelong career at Bolhão.

Maria Castro Pereira is
the third generation of
women in her family to
take on the art of working
with pork products.

At three years old, Maria Olinda Remísio Pinto was already at the market with her mother, who ran a stand similar to the one she has today.

Beef jerky lovers might easily understand this Portuguese passion for cured meat. Like the dried beef beloved by Americans and Canadians, most *enchidos* will not only last through the apocalypse but are easily transportable. The convenience of a hunk of *chouriço* in a Portuguese farmer's pocket was, and still is, invaluable.

In the cities, these smokehouse delicacies appear in supermarket aisles, hang from tavern ceilings, and inspire restaurant recipes. In Bolhão, you can get your hands on many of these products by visiting one of its *salsicharias* (charcuteries). The art of making *enchidos* has ritually been passed down from mother to daughter, a cultural piece still evident inside the market, where most of the *salsicharias* are operated by women who effortlessly command a cleaver while carrying on a conversation.

The male counterpart to this female-run show is Salsicharia Leandro, where there's a bustle of testosterone behind the counter every day. Yet, if you peek past the lineup of suspended sausages and parade of white coats, you'll spot a dainty, focused woman discreetly managing the cash register. She and her husband not only run this shop but have a factory in neighboring Rio Tinto, which supplies the key ingredients to restaurants serving up the city's iconic sandwich, the *francesinha* (a.k.a heart attack on a plate). This sandwich requires top-notch *salsicha fresca* (fresh sausage) and *linguiça* (smoked sausage) to delight appetites, and Salsicharia Leandro specializes in both. "The secret to our success are the high standards we've maintained for our meats all of these years," says Victor Ferreira, the husband and spokesperson for the shop. "Our *salsicha* and *linguiça,* for example, are made the same as 50 years ago."

And there's nothing more traditional in Porto than gorging on a *francesinha*! This monstrous masterpiece of a sandwich consists of layers upon layers of deli meats, fresh and smoked sausage, and steak stacked between two fat slices of bread smothered in melted cheese and doused in a spicy and oh-so-flavorful tomato and beer gravy. As if that weren't enough, you can top it off with a fried egg. For the adventurous, throw on some piri-piri for an extra bite. The history of the *francesinha* is hotly debated, but the prevailing story is that an emigrant from both Belgium and France invented it upon returning to Porto in the 1950s, where he adapted the croque monsieur to Portuguese tastes. As the tale is told, the name *francesinha* (little frenchie) was a tribute to the sensuous air of a French woman, a contrast to the then-reserved nature of the Portuguese. Regardless of region, one of the common threads in all of Portugal's cuisine is the talent to create unlikely ingredient combinations to achieve gluttonous glory on the plate. In Porto, the *francesinha* is one of the most ubiquitous examples of this masterful mixing.

Women are the face of cured meat at Bolhão, but at Salsicharia Leandro, you'll be greeted by a masculine smile.

Unlike butcher shops that carry a variety of meats, *salsicharias* specialize solely in pork products. The exception to the rule is the *alheira*—the queen bee of Northern sausages (and our ultimate favorite) with a blend of succulent meats, spices, and bread. Loaded up with *alho* (garlic), hence its name, *alheira* is believed to have originated as a pork-free sausage invented by Portuguese Jews to thwart the Inquisition (see Bread on page 21). Pork versions are common these days, but if you can get your hands on an *alheira de caça* (game meat only, e.g., partridge, venison, wild boar, and hare), don't pass it up. As opposed to the common pâté-esque *alheira*, this type contains firm, earthy slivers of pulled meat. Before frying one up, use a needle to poke a few holes on each side, which allows the skin to expand instead of burst.

Most of the *salsicharias* inside the market have *alheira* as well as ingredients you might need for an intricate Northern pork recipe. From pig's ears and feet to pork belly and sausage casings, they have it all, including a few tricks up their sleeves. Here's one: lemon juice hardens pork, so squeeze an orange instead! Searching for samples? Swing by and enjoy a complimentary bite to help you get acquainted with their products.

Left to right:

Sausage casings hang from a structural pole; Porto's cholesterol bomb *francesinha* **at A. Cunha 2.**

One of the top Northern *presuntos* (dry-cured ham) comes from the Barroso region.

OUR FAVORITES

Butelo

If gnawing on a smoky rib is your idea of pure gluttony, then multiply that experience by thousands of tiny bones tightly compressed with campfire aromas. May we introduce the *butelo* or *chouriça de ossos* (bone sausage)? Pig's bladder, tripe, or stomach is stuffed with the spare ribs, feather bones, and cartilage left over once the "best" meat has been picked over for premium sausages, leading to the creation of this cured flavor bomb. Boiled for about two hours, the *butelo* is traditionally served with sun-dried lima bean husks called *casulas*. Undoubtedly an ugly duckling dish, it's rustic richness in your mouth—just have plenty of floss handy to stand up to the mounds of chipped meat. Warning: *butelo* is a choking hazard for the wee ones.

Chouriço

The everyday smoked sausage of Portugal is the *chouriço*, which is sliced thinly for sandwiches or thickly for starters. Sometimes it's boiled, other times it's grilled. It's thrown into stews, casseroles, and even soups. Certain villages lace the meat with *mel* (honey), get creative with blood (resulting in *morcela de sangue*), or toss in tons more red wine than usual, equaling *chouriço de vinho*, which can easily be found at the market for a deeply flavored treat. And though you might be tempted to ask for it Spanish style, *chorizo*, that second accented *ç* in *chouriço* actually sounds like an *s*, so say "sho-REE-soo" instead. In terms of taste, the Portuguese version of this sausage is smokier than the Spanish or Mexican, which are spicier. Generally, fatty pork bits are seasoned with paprika, pepper, cumin, cloves, garlic, and red wine before being stuffed into casings that are smoked for several weeks.

Presunto

What *jamón* is to Spain, *presunto* (cured ham) is to Portugal. These sublimely cured hog legs hang from tavern ceilings and adorn restaurant tables, exposing just enough flesh to create instant salivation. One buttery slice of a whisper-thin *presunto de Barroso* and your knees will buckle. But these premium products tend to be reserved for the gourmet shops lining the market, while items better fit for a family budget are widely offered by the *salsicharias* within. In many cases vendors, like Maria Olinda Remísio Pinto from Salsicharia Lindinha, will purchase an entire leg and slice or dice the meat for individual, vacuum-sealed packets. For this quintessential nurturer, who spent her formative years in the village of Vila Nova de Foz Côa helping with her family's *fumeiro*, it's not about high-end prices; it's about flavor.

Salsicha Fresca

Don't expect traces of anise or fennel in Portuguese fresh sausage, as you'll commonly find in Italian American versions popular on U.S. breakfast menus. Portuguese sausages reflect the culture's love of tangy marinades deepened by droves of garlic, wine, vinegar, pepper, and cilantro, parsley, or oregano. Portuguese kids are often found with a plate of *salsicha frita* (fried sausage) and eggs sunny-side up, perfect for dipping their homemade fries. These tasty sausages are also commonly tossed in rice with peas, mixed with spaghetti, or wrapped in *couve lombarda* (savoy-style cabbage). Easy, quick, and delicious!

Toucinho

Sold *fresco* (fresh), *salgado* (salted), or *fumado* (smoked, which equals thick bacon), this hunk of decadent pork belly brings the Portuguese a bevy of blissful moments. It shows up as chunks in stews and soups; thinly sliced as *entremeada* on summer grills; and in bite-size pieces called *torresmos*, deep-fried to the point of being crunchy. In rural parts, the old-schoolers have been known to rub it on fireplace-toasted bread as a substitute for butter or olive oil. If you enjoy spreading bone marrow on your bread, you'll adore this flavorsome experience.

CHEESE

Alongside its rustic brethren of cured meats and olives, cheese completes the holy trinity of nibbles on the Portuguese table. Whether it's the cow-cheese wheels from the Azorean islands or the oozy rounds from the goats and sheep grazing the mountains on the mainland, every region in Portugal has its own artisanal *queijo* (cheese).

Ranging from *fresco* or *requeijão* (fresh) and *amanteigado* (buttery) to *curado* (cured) and *velho* (aged), there's plenty to experiment with as you travel through this tiny country's dramatically diverse terrain. In the Center region, you'll discover the country's most celebrated cheese, the Serra da Estrela, named after Portugal's highest mountain range. A popular destination for skiing and hiking, the mountain's charming lodges are also the ideal setting to spoon out buttery cheese onto crusty rye bread while a blazing fireplace cozies the room. In Porto, you'll easily find Serra cheese, but for an authentic taste of the North pick up Terrincho from the Trás-os-Montes and Alto Douro, which is made with milk from the Churra, an ancient breed of sheep also known as Terrincha. Though the Center and South offer a significantly wider variety of cheeses, Terrincho shouldn't be an afterthought. Cured and aged for a minimum of 30 days, and up to 90 days for *velho* status, look for a cheese with a rusty orange rub of *pimentão* (red pepper paste). Despite its thick encasement, inside the cheese is smooth and creamy yet firm, with a spicy nuttiness. For extra tang, seek out Terrincho cured in wooden barrels filled with *centeio* (rye)—a terrific pairing with *broa*.

As with the protected designation of origin (DOC) in wine, olive oil and cheese are stamped DOP to guarantee that they're produced within a demarcated region using traditional methods and ingredients. The labels also contain the name of the city or town of origin. But don't turn a blind eye to cheeses without DOP status, as they can be outstanding. The key is to experiment until your taste buds fall in love!

And if you're wondering what type of cheese is in that *tosta mista* pressed sandwich you see every Portuguese ordering at the café? Called Flamengo (cow's milk), it's Portugal's version of sliced cheese, modeled after the Dutch Edam. If you want to kick your *tosta mista* up a notch, grab a hunk of Limiano cheese from the city of Ponte de Lima in Minho—it's a higher-quality Flamengo than what's available at most supermarkets. You can find both Terrincho and Limiano at the Manteigaria do Bolhão—the kitschy kiosk on the mezzanine that's an ode to the artisanal butter shops that once dotted Porto—at the cheese vendor on the ground floor, or at the *mercearias* (specialty grocery stores) on the streets encircling the market.

A rustic display of cured
meats and cheeses at the
specialty shop Comer
e Chorar por Mais.

CHAPTER 7

PASTRIES & COFFEE

The *pastel de nata* (egg custard tart) is such a strong symbol for Portugal around the globe that politicians have dubbed it an international ambassador for the country.

I F YOU'RE EAGER to go native, step into one of the many *pastelarias* or *confeitarias* (cafés or pastry shops) blanketing Portugal's landscape. These caffeine temples are so entrenched in the culture that you can just about blindfold yourself and throw a stone in any one direction and nail an espresso cup! Why so many? Because for most of southern Europe, it's the place where neighbors, workers, friends, and family can belly up to the bar and feel at home, not just once, but several times throughout the day. A 15-minute escape from the grind, paired with a creamy café and a flaky pastry, is the pure essence of the Mediterranean. Cafés are the region's refueling stations for the soul!

Inside Bolhão, bread vendors happily provide you with a traditional pastry or biscuit, but to truly live and breathe the vibrancy of café culture in Portugal go explore the winding streets surrounding the market. Porto boasts some of the most elegant cafés in the world with places like Majestic Café and Confeitaria do Bolhão. These alluring cafés transport you to a bygone era with pretty confections and rich coffees that linger on your palate. If you're visiting Porto, it's a must on your list.

Beyond satisfying your sugar fix, Portuguese sweets feed the imagination with their decadent ancestry. As implied by the name, there are monastic ties to Portugal's *doçaria conventual* (convent sweets). The beloved egg custard tart—*pastel de Belém* in the original factory in Lisbon and *pastel de nata* elsewhere—is believed to have been born out of a nun's need to liquidate an overstock of egg yolks. With endless gifts of chickens and eggs from grateful farmers, nuns cleverly used egg whites as starch to stiffen their habits, while friars transformed them into a filtering agent to refine wine. With their basins overflowing with leftover yolks, the nuns whipped up dozens of sweets to sell. Coincidentally,

In Lisbon, an espresso shot is a *bica*. In Porto, it's a *cimbalino*, a term derived from the first espresso machines in Portugal, branded La Cimbali. Still, most Portuguese simply ask for a café.

this was a time when Portugal received an influx of sugar from its colony of Brazil, the perfect recipe for a rising pastry industry. In tribute to this holy history, several of these pastries have quirky religious names, such as *toucinho do céu* (bacon from heaven), *papos-de-anjos* (angel's chin), and *barriga de freiras* (nun's belly), to name a mere few. Guess you could say that Portuguese pastries are indeed divine!

One of our favorites is the *pão de ló de Ovar*, which is unique among a series of *pão de ló* (Portuguese sponge cake) recipes because of its molten center. Though it requires only three ingredients—eggs, sugar, and flour—the secret lies in the amount of humidity and fluff achieved by underbaking the batter. The Ovar version is one of the hardest *pão de ló* recipes to bake because it requires a significant

amount of coddling. "It's an intimate process," explains Sandra Dolores Pais Cruz, whose family owns the Cruz company. While scooping batter into hundreds of ceramic bowls with her hand, she laments about poor representations of the cake outside of Ovar. "My concern," she says, "is that people who bake this cake outside of our local shops may not do it justice, giving it a bad reputation." Unlike some cloyingly sweet versions of this cake, Cruz's is balanced and delightful! Though we highly recommend visiting the prettily tiled *pão de ló* boutiques in Ovar, a city edging into the Center region, you can also find this kind of cake at restaurants in Porto. Sandra suggests pairing it with a tawny Port—the older the better—as well as *espumante* and Vinho Verde.

Explore O Gaveto's tawny Port (left) wine selection when savoring their oozy *pão de ló* (right).

In the far north, there's another prestigious sponge cake that graces the dessert tables of the royal Casa de Bragança (vestiges of Portugal's monarchical past) called *pão de ló de Margaride*, from the town of Felgueiras. Though both these cakes share the moniker of *pão de ló*, they're entirely different creatures. While the Ovar cake is smooth on the outside and oozy on the inside, the Margaride version is more of a bundt cake that's slightly denser inside and out. Porto loves its *pão de ló*—as do the bread vendors at Bolhão—providing ample opportunities to taste test your way through the city.

Pão de ló sits regally in the display case at Confeitaria do Bolhão.

This sacred love affair with eggs speaks to harsher days for the Portuguese when rural families trekked long distances on foot to sell freshly laid dozens at fairs, generating what was often their sole source of income. When sales were weak, they returned to their country kitchens to whip up gigantic *pão de ló* cakes that made good use of the mounds of leftover eggs. So next time a Portuguese recipe calls for 20 yolks, you'll understand why!

Though egg creams are the centerpiece of pastries in Portugal, you'll detect a few other influences as well. For instance, honey and nuts are remnants of the Moorish occupation of the Iberian Peninsula. Seek out *broa de mel* for traces of walnuts and honey, or the caramel and almond cream of *baba de camelo*. Yes, that means "camel's drool"! But don't let the funky name deter you. When the sugar is balanced and the cream drips from your spoon with the infusion of almond crunchies, you've struck gold with this dessert. There's a French air to some of the pastries with names clearly pointing to the Napoleonic invasions. The Portuguese interpretation of the French *mille-feuille*, for instance, is called a *mil-folhas* in Lisbon, but in Porto, it's called a *napoleão*. There is in fact a *mil-folhas* in Porto, but it's entirely different and also goes by the name of *russo folhado* (see Our Favorites on page 200). Indeed, Portugal has a million different names for its products depending on the region—it's the perfect way to keep you conversing with the locals.

Try pairing this pastry experience with Portugal's deeply robust coffee. Though a break to snack on something sweet is an integral part of the Portuguese lifestyle, nothing is as ritualistic as indulging in darkly roasted espresso. Do the Portuguese need that much of a caffeine boost to get through their days? Not quite—it's the addictive flavor cultivated from centuries of perfecting the art of coffee making that they need. During the Age of Discovery, most of Portugal's colonies were some of the world's top coffee bean–growing regions, many of which maintained a thriving trade connection with the Portuguese. And like so many of the other foods that the Portuguese discovered and helped spread to other countries, coffee went global! In the 1700s, Francisco de Mello Palheta was sent to French Guiana to fetch a coffee plant that initiated the first coffee bean production by the Portuguese in Brazil. Throughout the rest of the 18th century, Brazilian coffee beans were hauled back to Portugal to satiate the parched noblemen. Eventually, the Portuguese art of roasting coffee gave rise to the very first public cafés in Lisbon, which instantaneously turned into hubs for cultural debate. Many of the legendary Portuguese coffee companies that were founded in that era are still in operation today. But no other café embodies the Brazilian connection more than Lisbon's Café A Brasileira, where the iconic statue

Portuguese confectionary techniques were introduced to Japan during the Age of Discovery, including kasutera *sponge cake* (pão de ló) *and* keiran somen *egg threads* (fios de ovos).

Like their European cousins, the Portuguese adore their custard puddings. *Leite crème*, the coveted dessert of Minho, combines milk, lemon peel, and cinnamon to create a luscious cream covered in candied caramel.

of the Portuguese poet Fernando Pessoa sits. Defunct for years, Porto's own Café A Brasileira has been restored to its original glory as a four-star hotel.

Other ingredients that bind sweets across the regions are lemons, cinnamon, fortified wines—and even bacon! The grand city of Braga, where there seem to be as many convents as there are pastry shops, is home to the *pudim Abade de Priscos*, a.k.a the "bacon pudding." This custard embodies the essence of Portuguese desserts with its triad of citrus, cinnamon, and Port. Though it resembles flan, there's absolutely no milk in it. It's a small dose of lard that provides the silky texture. Believed to have been invented in the 19th century by Manuel Rabelo, an abbot (of course!) who was from the town of Priscos and had an epicurean gift, this dessert became a favorite of Braga's nobility and continues to be a highlight on the city's menus.

Olive oil has also seeped its way into desserts; however, butter is the hallmark of Portuguese pastries and a favorite to spread on a *torrada* (toast). Historically, cities were dotted with high-quality *leitarias* (dairy shops) and *manteigarias* (butter shops), but it was the Azores islands that were known for their insanely decadent butter—customarily shipped to the mainland to be savored. The island import remains a favorite of the Portuguese, but on the mainland, Lacticínios das Marinhas in the town of Esposende (off coastal Minho) produces one of the country's top craft butters, Manteiga Marinhas.

Made with lard, egg yolks, and Port wine, *pudim à Abade de Priscos* is pure heaven.

Café napkins are great for wrapping around a buttery pastry because of their top-notch fat absorption, but they don't work well for much else.

Left to Right:

Milk and dark chocolate *línguas de gato* at Arcádia; Arcádia storefront; tray of freshly baked Valongo biscuits at Paupério.

If you adore handcrafted chocolate—infused with everything from olive oil and wine to fruits and nuts—dip into one of the many luxurious chocolate shops throughout the city. At the top of the list: Arcádia. Founded in 1933, Arcádia is considered one of Porto's top chocolatiers, acclaimed for its milk and dark chocolate *línguas de gato* (cat tongues), slivers of chocolate seasoned with delicate sweetness.

Tantalizing your taste buds with sugary delights isn't the only reason to visit Porto's pastry shops and cafés—step inside for the décor. Beyond the sweet spots encircling the market, stroll a few blocks south to the exotic Café Guarany on the magnificent Aliados Square. For hardcore dairy lovers, head to the Praça de Guilherme Gomes Fernandes plaza in the Baixa (Downtown). Historically known

for hosting the *feira do pão* (bread fair), the plaza is now colloquially called the *praça do pão* (bread square). There, you'll discover two Porto institutions: Leitaria da Quinta do Paço, a creamery, and Padaria Ribeiro, a bakery. For more than 200 years, Padaria Ribeiro has been serving up scrumptious pastries, including Valongo biscuits (also available at the bread vendors inside Bolhão) with coffee, tea, or Port wine.

Though the vintage paper bags and tin boxes these biscuits come in are splendid, there's nothing quite like visiting the quaint town where the biscuits are produced. Less than 20 minutes from Porto, you can be in the Paupério biscuit factory, one of the oldest producers in Valongo. Since 1874, they've been serving up homemade cookies that have enticed even the most curmudgeonly of grandmothers.

Artisanal bakers churn out hundreds of scrumptious biscuits daily on Paupério's vintage machinery.

One of the perks of visiting Paupério's storefront is watching these pastry experts handpick assorted biscuits for their grandchildren. "I only buy the ones they like," exclaims a woman buttoned up in a blue silk blouse. "That way there's no waste." Of course! If there are two things we've learned about the Portuguese by now, it's that one, waste is an utter abomination, and two, that tradition is profoundly sacred.

At Paupério, ancient recipes and a personalized selection process play a huge role in maintaining tradition. It's so personal that one woman individually inspects each and every biscuit by hand before putting them in their packaging. For half a century, she has worked with the company, manually sorting an average of 5,000 biscuits a day.

"I'm the fifth generation," says owner Eduardo Sousa, who is working on a museum inside the factory and on ways to open its artisanal operation to the public. "Now, I'll be passing the business down to my daughters." He's eager to give a new generation of Portuguese the chance to be part of the Paupério family. "To work at Paupério you don't need to have any baking experience; what you need is good, human qualities."

Just as with Bolhão, what we cherish about the people sprinkling Porto with sugar is their rooted spirit of preservation and soulful core.

Did you know that the Portuguese originally discovered *chá* (tea) in their former colony of Macau? It wasn't until the fair Princess Catarina of Bragança married the adulterous King Charles II of England that tea became synonymous with Britain. Still, the steamy beverage of choice in Portugal is coffee.

OUR FAVORITES

Jesuíta

Beyond *jesuíta*'s monastic name, we're convinced the Jesuits were sly in their creation of this flaky beast, because after one bite your romantic prospects will be nonexistent! Why? Roughly the size of your head, this pastry is incredibly messy to maneuver into your mouth. With every nibble, brace yourself for a carnage of crumbs all over your clothing. It's also impossibly dry when not paired with a beverage—but absolutely blissful with a tawny Port. Despite its quirks, we're completely addicted to this odd, triangular puff pastry coated with a decadent cinnamon meringue crust. If you can get your hands on a *jesuíta* filled with cinnamon egg cream, it's cause for a hallelujah!

Éclair

We know what you're thinking—yes, the éclair is French. But since Napoleon had the nerve to invade Porto, the Portuguese turned the trespassing into a point of pastry pride by twisting the French classics. Porto's version is injected with decadent whipped cream and drizzled with a variety of toppings, including white and dark chocolate, lemon, berries, caramel, and Port. It was created by the Leitaria da Quinta do Paço in the 1920s, a Northern pioneer in bottling and distributing milk to households. Before it started its business, women in Porto distributed milk from heavy pitchers carried on top of their heads. More than just a place to enjoy one of the best éclairs we've ever devoured, Leitaria's (Baixa) location breathes history with black-and-white photos of its shop's early years displayed tastefully on its walls.

Mil-Folhas

Make sure that when ordering a *mil-folhas* in Porto you're not actually asking for the *napoleão*. Throughout most of Portugal, the *mil-folhas* resembles the French *mille-feuille*, glazed in chocolate ganache with cream perforated into pockets of puffed sheets. But in Porto, the *mil-folhas* is a load of cream sandwiched between puffed squares with a generous coating of powdered sugar and a cross designed out of cinnamon. There's that monastic tie-in again! Also called a *russo folhado*, this pastry is perfect to cut in half and split with a friend. Its creaminess and cinnamon beg for a velvety coffee.

Café

A shot of espresso (two to three ounces) is the most ubiquitous style of coffee you'll find in Portugal and is consumed in huge quantities—we're talking three to four times a day! It is often paired with a *pão simples* or *pão caseiro* (crusty rolls) or a pastry. But if this isn't enough to soothe a late-night hangover, double it with a *café duplo* (double) or a *café cheio* (full). The reverse is also true: if you simply need a taste without the commitment, ask for a *café curto* (half shot).

Pingado

If pure unadulterated coffee isn't your . . . ahem . . . cup of tea, then why not add a drop or two of milk? Served in an espresso cup, it's an excellent way to tame the intensity of the rich espresso. Most people will know this as a macchiato. For something even creamier than a *pingado*, ask for a *pingo*. It's served with a 50-50 proportion of milk and coffee in an espresso cup.

Galão

If your body craves more milk than coffee, then perhaps the creamy *galão* is the best fit for you. This warm latte-esque beverage is served in a tall glass and made with one part espresso and three parts milk. For an even milkier version, try a *galão clarinho* (light).

CONCLUSION

The Future of Bolhão

"The value of things is not the time they last, but the intensity with which they occur. That is why there are unforgettable moments and unique people!"

—FERNANDO PESSOA

SHOWERED BY A prism of orange sunlight, a slender woman with scarlet tresses casually leans against a rugged stone wall inside a small warehouse and breathes in the afternoon calm. Like the handful of produce stands inside this shared space in the Massarelos neighborhood (two miles from Bolhão), hers is rich with fresh, locally sourced vegetables and fruit. Thick, vibrant bushels of kale, cabbage, and lettuce rise up from the floor around her, accentuating her earthy farm-girl feel. Tânia Dias is radiant.

Squinting against the bright light, she pushes an unruly lock behind her ear and sings, "Now, what can I do for you?"

After a lengthy conversation about the magnificent quality and diversity of the fruit she has on offer from the Douro, we point to a sign hanging loosely above the freezer reading "Mercado do Bom Sucesso de Agramonte," inquiring about the relationship between this modest space and the posh Bom Sucesso Market in Porto's business district.

"Oh that," Tânia says with a slight wave of her hand. "No, there's no current relationship between the new Bom Sucesso Market and this market. It's only because this is the spot where folks came to sell

Jean-Marc Vuillaume is a street performer at Bolhão, entertaining the masses with his musical marionettes.

Founded in 1917 by
António Rodrigues Reis,
A Pérola do Bolhão is
a homey delicatessen
specializing in cured
meats and cheeses.

their goods when Bom Sucesso Market went into renovations. Now, it's just a few of us here, and I'm not even from this market. I've only been here a few months. I'm from Bolhão!"

That one word, Bolhão, is like a geyser of emotions. It's a force that explodes from the ground causing a wake of memories and sadness. In tears, Tânia wraps her arms around her waist to ease her sorrow.

Long gaps of silence are interrupted by gasping breaths of apologies. "I'm sorry," she says, "I . . . I just want to go home [referring to Bolhão]. I know I can't change the past, and I need to accept that it's over, but I want to go home." With the tip of her forefinger, she softly wipes away a rogue tear only to find three more in its place. "My friends, my family, everything was at Bolhão. It used to be so full of life, but now . . . it's over."

We can't even write this without crying ourselves. We embraced this project precisely because of the neglected souls inside Bolhão's crumbling walls, the people that the world has deemed antiquated. These people have chipped nails, dirt-lined palms, and frayed aprons because they bring us the food we often take for granted. While we jump in our swanky electric cars to get our gluten-free bread and perfectly polished chicken breasts, the vendors at Bolhão are living what we bullshit about in hip cafés. They're practicing what we're preaching.

They're interconnected.

Despite Mother Nature's tantrums of hurricane winds, frigid rain, and suffocating temperatures, Bolhão's vendors (past and present) have braved the elements every day because the market is their home. It's where they met their first loves, watched their fathers fall ill, and ate their first *chouriços*. It's where their grandmothers carted in vegetables on foot, and where they sang their first Fado songs. It's where generations of local families have spent their weekends shopping, eating, and socializing under an open-air canopy swirling with seagulls. It's gritty, it's colorful, it's real.

Needlessly rearranging the fat fruit behind her, Tânia takes a few minutes to compose herself. Turning with a fig in hand, she takes a bite, smirks, and nods—a playful push to carry on.

"We visited several cities to see markets . . . and the one element that Bolhão has that makes it special is the capacity of the vendors to be caring and empathic with their customers."

—Luís Mendonça, designer

"Would you go back to Bolhão if conditions improved and you could make money?" we ask. Tânia blares out an unequivocal "Yes," followed by sudden concern. "I would love to go back, but then again, maybe it won't be the same. Many of my friends are gone, but still . . . I want to be there, I want to be back in Bolhão."

Tânia isn't alone. There's an entirely new generation that's feeling Bolhão's pull—and they're refusing to let go. These Bolhão heirs are emboldened by a passion to move businesses forward with the same dogged determination and wit as their ancestors. In fact, there's an onslaught of vibrant youth searching for a space of their own, fueled by the same entrepreneurial spirit that turned Porto into a case study for success during the Troika economic crisis of 2010. This new generation is starved for the maternal meaningfulness of the market as much as the market is aching for their fresh blood and enlivening ideas.

Hugo Silva and his wife, Patrícia Sousa, are at the forefront of positive change inside the market with their modern wine and *petiscos* (small bites) bar called The Bolhão Wine House. The concept was considered radical and avant-garde to many vendors inside Bolhão, but it has proven to be worth its weight in gold.

"For years, City Hall only spoke about rebuilding the market from scratch; essentially, to completely demolish it and start over," explains Hugo. "What we wanted to do is demonstrate that the market can be renewed and restored in another way. That's what we've done with this space. We're a living example."

Hugo's grandmother Maria Albertina Sousa started selling flowers in the market alongside her mother in the 1930s. From across the river in Vila Nova de Gaia, Maria Albertina would haul baskets of fresh flowers by foot all the way to Bolhão. At the tender age of seven, this was no easy task, but the shrewd business skills she acquired allowed her to open two flower shops inside the market. In partnership with her daughter, the businesses thrived until 2006, when they were forced out due to both economic reasons and the structural demise of the market. Years later, Hugo petitioned the city to let him take over the title of his family's shop. His goal was to transform it into the successful bar it is today, while retaining the core message of the market: support businesses inside Bolhão. The epitome of hyperlocal!

"Look across from us. There's a flower shop. Next to us is a cheese shop. And down there is a produce stand. In every other market, we would all be sectioned off with like products, which doesn't make any sense. By being mixed together, we can support each other," argues Hugo, who buys his pâtés, canned sardines, cheeses, and olives from the vendors surrounding his charming bar, where *petiscos* and a glass of wine are served atop repurposed wine barrels. He also encourages his patrons to grab a slice of *broa* from the bread goddesses inside the market and a hunk of fragrant *chouriço* from the *salsicharias* to pair with a glass of Douro red at his place. If he doesn't offer a particular product, and patrons can get it from another vendor at the market, he's all for it.

Part of Bolhão's new generation, Hugo Silva and his wife, Patrícia Sousa, are shaking things up at the market with unprecedented business concepts.

This young couple embodies the future of Bolhão, a spirit of hope seasoned with a sense of pride for the past. All Hugo and Patrícia have ever asked for is that the city give the market a chance to thrive with the support it needs to be vibrant again. And for the first time in decades, their wish may come true.

As of this book's writing, the city announced that it would be moving the vendors to a temporary market inside the La Vie shopping center on Rua de Fernandes Tomás, within walking distance to Bolhão, where they would remain for the projected two-year period of renovations. Though it won't be entirely business as usual without the majesty of the building, the charismatic vendors, their fresh products, and sense of community will surely lure over customers yearning for their weekly dose of gossip and the healing powers of the men and women of Bolhão.

The proposed project features an open-air market with the same look and feel as before, but with significantly upgraded conditions. Everything from plumbing to electricity will be overhauled to ensure vendors have the basic tools to do their jobs well. Stands will be outfitted with modern equipment

The grand staircase is an architectural symbol of the past and an invitation to a bright, new future inside Bolhão Market.

and protection against the rain, restaurants will receive adequate kitchens, security guards will be on staff, and a subway stop will offer direct access to the market.

As for the vendors, city officials claim that they want nothing more than to keep them on to nurture and retain the essence of the market. According to Francisco Rocha Antunes, consultant on the committee that manages the renovation project for Bolhão Market, "This is not a tourist-oriented market; it's a fresh-food market aimed at local residents. So we're doing everything we can to ensure the existing retailers have ample opportunities to succeed as they are. We want to empower them, not change them. We need to retain a collective example of what is the soul of the city."

Though we're hoping that the city can meet its objective of maintaining as many of the existing vendors as possible in the renovated market, we know in our hearts that some of the vendors we've made friendships with will move on. Whether they retire, or are gently prodded to transform their stands into something more in line with the project's theme of fresh foods and flavor, change is inevitable. And it has already begun as some of the market's most emblematic vendors left before the makeshift market's location was announced in 2017.

From the moment we started this project, we understood that there would be casualties throughout a seemingly endless saga about the future of the market, igniting in us this sense of urgency to capture the stories of the people of Bolhão—a mission we assigned to ourselves in hopes of highlighting the importance of the market beyond its architecturally stunning building. Our loyalty has been to the human heritage inside, to the treasures buried in the vendors' memories. Lest someone recorded them as we did, they would be lost over time.

Our desire is that through this book, people can understand why these vendors and their loyal customers fought tooth and nail with endless petitions and protests to keep the market from falling into the wrong hands.

"After more than 100 interviews with people in and outside of the market, we were able to get a solid understanding of what's needed, what's important, and how we can shift the market into something that has heart and soul for both the vendors and their customers," says Luís Mendonça, designer with the architectural team that's working on the renovation project for Bolhão. "We visited several cities to see markets in Barcelona, Madrid, Valencia, Lisbon, Paris, etc., and the one element that Bolhão has that makes it special is the capacity of the vendors to be caring and empathic with their customers. They want the customers to be happy, to feel something in that moment of connection. We do too."

We vicariously lived Bolhão's poetic existence through the vendors' stories, ebbing and flowing with their low and high tides. We witnessed the degradation of their setting, tasted their frustration, and shuddered from their pain. If we could have snapped our fingers together, we would have created a market they would feel proud of, a place they could have safely called home without years of delays.

We would like to emphasize that having a sense of pride and hope isn't just vital for the vendors, it's critical for the community as a whole. Like Tânia, burning with a desire to return to Bolhão, we all

Just 10 minutes south of Bolhão Market, the São Bento train station shares many of the market's late neoclassical features, as both were built around the same time.

want to be part of something bigger than ourselves. By generating interest for Bolhão, we're hoping to do more than pay homage to a traditional market, we're pushing to preserve every link in the food cycle to help forge a more meaningful future for everyone. We see Bolhão as a path to getting our souls and hearts closer to what we've been straying from all of these years.

In the end, our wish is that this book will do its small part in reviving respect for markets like our beloved Bolhão.

Traces of the country's dominant Roman Catholic faith are strong inside the market.

AFTERWORD
BY RUI PAULA

"Books that highlight the best of what's made in Portugal, in a region, in a market like Bolhão, will not only inspire people to come live and breathe our story, but they'll help us appreciate what we already have."

—CHEF RUI PAULA

I **WAS BORN IN** the North of Portugal, and those closest to me are well aware of how proud I am of this heritage. I express it in my food, my language, and the way I interact with the world. There's absolutely nothing I would defend more than my culture.

I love the North because of its authenticity, its simplicity, and its passion. A basic soup will be infused with the flavors and aromas of our past, carried on from generation to generation. It's a level of pride and dedication to our roots that's not only inspiring but soulful, as rightfully seen in our wines. They're unique, diverse, and crafted by people who genuinely love to drink them.

The Nortenhos (people of the North) are extremely easygoing and cheerful, yet carry a fervent spirit of independence and pride that can't merely be expressed in words. If you truly want to understand us, sit down and share a bottle of wine with us, savor our home-cooked meals, and take in our scenery.

This free and open spirit is ingrained in every tile and every vendor inside Bolhão Market. Since 1839, Bolhão has become a fundamental symbol of the warmth of an entire region—the soul of the North. Its close-knit community of passionate vendors, combined with its exceptional products, is a rarity in our modern times. Even today, it's impossible for the Portuguese to leave the market without something in our bags. It's where we feel intrinsically connected to our culture and to ourselves.

Today, Bolhão has once again become a topic of conversation, because fortunately we're returning to local products that offer authentic flavors and colors—all of which can be found inside Bolhão. I speak of a space with a grand mezzanine that overlooks a bustling Old World bazaar, a place where you feel the personality and soul of everything and everyone inside it. Bolhão embodies the purest expression of the North!

Inside Bolhão, people instantly feel that they're in Porto—they see it and live it. It's a place with a vibrant personality and raw sensations. And though Bolhão is old, it certainly isn't irrelevant.

As chefs, we cannot innovate if there aren't places like Bolhão in the world. Without products rooted in tradition and a sense of place, we would all be cooking the same dishes. What distinguishes countries, chefs, and cuisines are their unique ingredients—this is a fundamental rule for success.

I can't stress enough how important it is to celebrate our culture, to promote our talents, and to pass down our passions to new generations—because there are certain things in life that are bigger than any of us. Books that highlight the best of what's made in Portugal, in a region, in a market like Bolhão, will not only inspire people to come live and breathe our story, but they'll help us appreciate what we already have.

To me, Bolhão is more than a market. It's our soul. It's our roots. And without roots, nothing grows.

Considered to be an indispensable reference to modern Portuguese cuisine, and distinguished with a Michelin star, **Chef Rui Paula**'s dishes reveal the memory of his origins in Northern Portugal. His restaurants include DOC in the Douro Valley, DOP, and the starred Casa de Chá da Boa Nova in Porto. His most recent project, Terraço, has just launched in the Tivoli Avenida Liberdade hotel in Lisbon.

ACKNOWLEDGMENTS

WHEN WE EMBARKED on this writing adventure together, we couldn't have imagined the emotional roller-coaster ride that would ensue. Word to the wise: whatever you start with will surely not be the product you end with. Books take on a life of their own! They consume your every waking moment, absorb your life force, and bring to light any and all weaknesses stored within—hello inner naysayer! In short, writing a book is both tantalizing and diabolical, which is why it's so important to share our appreciation and endless gratitude with those who never let us give up.

From our dear family and friends that stood by our side through every single minute of this process—witnessing our defeats and victories—to our collaborators tirelessly checking and confirming each piece of information to make this book the best it could be, and to the talented professionals that jumped in last minute to provide invaluable feedback, pausing their lives to give it to us—we're humbled by your generosity and wisdom. There's no acknowledgment page that could ever fully capture our gratitude, but know that we couldn't have done it without you.

A tremendous thank-you to our team! But especially to Ryan Opaz, not only for your evocative photos, but for your tireless support and encouragement to help us make this book a reality. You believed in us before we ever could, enduring our extreme pendulum swings, radio silences, and constant self-doubt. Thank you from the bottom of our hearts! To Catarina Gonçalves, Cláudia Ferreira Marques, and Ana Correia for your invaluable research, calls, and scheduling; Andreia Barbosa for the last-minute research; Júlia Melo Kemper, Filomena André, and their team at Melo Kemper Advogados for your generous guidance; Catherine Fisher Rodrigues for going out of your way every time we needed it; Charyliz Rodriguez, Juna Wesley, and José Miguel Carvalho Cardoso for your artistic input and contributions; Mark Tafoya and Chef André Antunes for unraveling the mysteries of our recipes; and last but certainly not least, to the insightful reviewers André Apolinário of Taste Porto Food Tours and George Reis, as well as our rock star editors: Jessica Rosero, Denise Costa, and Jeff Theodore.

Thank you to Catavino, the place where this all started and where we plundered for the in-depth research our talented contributors bring to the website every day.

To our agent Maxwell P. Sinsheimer and Jessica Easto at Agate Publishing, we couldn't be more appreciative of your support in launching our book internationally. And to Bárbara Simões, formerly at Oficina do Livro, for embracing a risky project with absolutely no caveats. Without believers like you many unconventional books would never see the light of day. Thank you all!

A special thank-you to Paulo Nolasco for your love, patience, support, and ingenious sense of humor through each high and low. Without your generosity and flexibility, this would never ever have happened! The sweetest of thank-yous to Mica Douro Opaz, a.k.a King Sunflower, for hanging in there with us when you should have been chasing roosters in the park! To Maria Luísa Batista Barros Lopes and Carla Alexandra Barros Cruz Silva at Café 3emes, who perpetually showered us in love and attention, as well as the entire staff at Externato São João de Brito, who rolled with every last-minute change and forgotten lunch we threw at you. You're incredible!

To Cornell and Patti Anderson, thank you so much for lending us your amazing eagle eyes. Maria do Céu and José Luís Andresson for your love, gracious chauffeuring, hospitality, delicious food, and indispensable little green car that made it possible for us to get a huge chunk of research accomplished; Julia Nicole Andresson for showing us love with your welcome drawings and sharing your time with our work when we should have been dipping our toes in the rivers—we'll make it up to you one day; Manuel Luís Andresson for loving Portugal as deeply as we do; and Jennifer Pensiero for the healing.

Thank you Benvinda and João Diogo for whipping up an unexpected dinner for us in minutes, your squishy sandwich hugs, a place to sleep, and a trunk brimming with plump tomatoes; Nelson, Anabela, André, and Daniela Diogo for an infinite readiness to help with any request; Maria Zélia and Victor Nunes for your connections at the doctor. Thank you to Lucinda and João Farinha for a comfy bed and TONS of pampering; Florbela and João Ribeiro for sweet dinners and train tips; Bruno Caldeira and Ruben Pêgo for all the rides and intellectual conversations; Cátia Pêgo for checking in on our progress every single day for three years; Carla Andresson for the good vibes and research; and José Cancela for banking advice. For taking the time to get us feedback from your publishing contacts, thank you Bruno Mariano and John Lawless. Thank you Rosa Gonçalves for the warmest of smiles each time we entered the market! And an enormous sisterly shout-out to Bernadette Wesley for eating *tripa enfarinhada* for the cause and a heartfelt thank-you for always genuinely caring for us.

For the insights, leads, and all-around support offered throughout this process, we want to thank Marion Nestle, Nelson Carvalheiro, Bill Bennett, Charles Metcalfe and Kathryn McWhirter, David Leite, Ana Patuleia Ortins, César Santos Silva, Sandra O'Loughlin, Matthew Glass, Steve Santos, Rochelle Ramos, Miguel Carvalho, Chef José Avillez, Chef Rui Paula, Chef Kiko Martins, Michael Furman of Coachbuilt Press, José Alberto Manoel Allen of Quinta de Vilar d'Allen, Rui Reigota of Cooks 4 Looks, José Manuel Lello of Livraria Lello, Pedro Poças Pintão of Poças Junior Port, Carlos Lucas of Magnum Wines, Pedro Pinto of 1912 Winemakers, Lazy Flavors: Taste & Explore, APTECE, Bento Amaral of IVDP, Fernando Leal and Paulo Costa of the Confraria da Broa de Avintes, Ana Ventura Miranda of the Arte Institute, and Kim Sawyer, president of TLSG and wife of the former U.S. ambassador to Portugal.

Without muses there's absolutely nothing, so we couldn't be more grateful for the inspiration we found inside Bolhão Market, Padaria Arminda & Neto, Confraria da Broa de Avintes, Flor dos Congregados, Padaria Central, Museu do Pão e do Vinho de Favaios, Município de Mirandela, Lota de Matosinhos, O Gaveto, O Paparico, Taberna de São Pedro, Restaurante O Lusitano, A Casa do Evaristo, Restaurante Bem-Me-Quer, Delicatum Braga, Turismo de Braga, Cantinho das Manas, Câmara Municipal de Gondomar, Turismo de Gondomar, Taste Porto Food Tours, A Cozinha do Manel, O Caraças, Paupério, Cruz Pão de Ló, Ovar Turismo, Leitaria da Quinta do Paço, the entire Quevedo family, Oliva & Co., Cantinho das Aromáticas, Cantinho do Avillez, and Câmara Municipal do Porto.

Lastly, we'd like to thank wine, chocolate, and Skype—our holy trinity. Without this trio we might not have made it out alive!

RESOURCES

BOOKS

Anderson, Jean. *The Food of Portugal*. New York: HarperCollins, 1994.

Carvalheiro, Nelson. *Viagens pelas Receitas de Portugal*. Évora: Caminho das Palavras, 2015.

Duarte, Frederico. Ferreira, Pedro. João, Rita. *Fabrico Próprio: o design da pastelaria semi-industrial portuguesa*. Self-published. 2nd ed., 2012.

Ingram, Christine. Shapter, Jennie. *The Best-Ever Book of Bread*. New York: Metro Books, 2010.

Leite, David. *The New Portuguese Table*. New York: Clarkson Potter, 2009.

Mendes, George. *My Portugal*. New York: Abrams, 2014.

Mirene. *Tesouro das Cozinheiras*. Porto: Porto Editora, 2000.

Modesto, Maria de Lourdes. *Cozinha Tradicional Portuguesa*. Lisboa: Babel, 2012.

Moreiras, Paulo. *Pão & Vinho*. Alfragide: Publicações Dom Quixote, 2014.

Ortins, Ana Patuleia. *Portuguese Homestyle Cooking*. Northampton, MA: Interlink, 2006.

Rosa-Limpo, Bertha. Brum do Canto, Jorge. Limpo Caetano, Maria Manuel. Alves Caetano, Nuno. O *Livro de Pantagruel*. Lisbon: Temas e Debates, 2014.

WEBSITES AND ARTICLES

Aldeiasortugal.pt
Asenhoradomonte.com
Avintes.net
Carnebarrosa.com
Catavino.net
Clubederodutores.continente.pt
Cm-gaia.pt/pt/
Cozinhatradicional.com
Dn.pt

Gastronomias.com
Leitaobairrada.com
Localporto.com
Minhaterra.pt
Monocle.com
Nelsoncarvalheiro.com
Porcobisaro.net/dados/index.php
Portoalities.com/en/
Portoenorte.pt/pt/

Portugal-aptece.com
Portugalnumclick.com
Publico.pt
Saltofportugal.com
Tasteporto.com
Trajesdeportugal.blogspot.com
Upmagazine-tap.com
Virgiliogomes.com

"10 Things They Eat in Portugal," Summer Whitford, https://www.thedailymeal.com/travel/10-things-they-eat-portugal

"Cultural Communities and Identities," New Bedford Whaling Museum, https://www.whalingmuseum.org/learn/research-topics/cultural-communities

"Fish Sauce: An Ancient Roman Condiment Rises Again," Deena Prichep, https://www.npr.org/sections/thesalt/2013/10/26/240237774/fish-sauce-an-ancient-roman-condiment-rises-again

"Portugal's Nazaré: A Beach Town with Traditions," Rick Steves, https://www.ricksteves.com/watch-read-listen/read/articles/nazare-a-beach-town-with-traditions

"Recipes: Chicken Vindaloo," *Saveur*, https://www.saveur.com/classic-chicken-vindaloo

INDEX

Numbers in **bold** indicate pages with photos.

ABOUT CATAVINO

Catavino, a boutique travel agency based in Porto with a focus on the food and wine of Portugal and Spain, sparked two writers and one photographer to transform their shared love for Portugal into a book.

ABOUT THE CONTRIBUTORS

Ryan Opaz

Gabriella Opaz is an award-winning speaker, writer, and consultant on storytelling and communication. Cofounder and co-owner of Catavino, she contributes to *Wine & Spirits Magazine*. Gabriella cofounded the Born Digital Wine Awards (BDWA), which celebrate responsible, diverse wine journalism around the globe, and was a TEDx Porto speaker in 2017. Born in Chicago, Gabriella now lives in Porto.

Jessica Rosero

Sonia Andresson Nolasco is a journalist, editor, and publicist who primarily works with food, wine, travel, and art organizations to promote Portugal. She resigned as a public relations director in Manhattan to join Catavino, immersing herself in Bolhão Market intermittently for two years to build the relationships that inspired the intimate portraits in the book. Born in Lisbon, Portugal, and raised in the Ironbound, Newark, a Portuguese enclave in New Jersey, Sonia now lives in West Chester, Pennsylvania.

Gabriella Opaz

Ryan Opaz is a photographer and knight of the Port Wine Brotherhood who has worked as a chef, butcher, art teacher, public speaker, and wine writer. As CEO of Catavino, which he cofounded with his wife, Gabriella, he has spent the last 12 years guiding people throughout Portugal, kindling their love for a country and people he cherishes.